HARRY STACK SULLIVAN'S CONCEPTS OF PERSONALITY DEVELOPMENT AND PSYCHIATRIC ILLNESS

Harry Stack Sullivan's Concepts of Personality Development and Psychiatric Illness

by

A. H. CHAPMAN, M.D.

*Visiting Lecturer, The Greater Kansas City Mental Health
Foundation. Formerly, Associate Clinical Professor of
Psychiatry, University of Kansas School of Medi-
cine, and Attending Psychiatrist, St. Mary's
Hospital, Menorah Medical Center and
Research Hospital and Medical
Center, Kansas City, Missouri*

and

MIRIAM C. M. S. CHAPMAN, M.D.

*Research Associate, The Greater Kansas
City Mental Health Foundation*

BRUNNER/MAZEL, *Publishers* • New York

Library of Congress Cataloging in Publication Data

Chapman, Arthur Harry, 1924-
  Harry Stack Sullivan's concepts of personality development and psychiatric illness.

  1. Sullivan, Harry Stack, 1892-1949.   2. Psychoanalysis.   3. Personality.
4. Personality in children.   5. Psychology, Pathological.   6. Interpersonal
relations.   I. Chapman, Miriam C. M. S., 1951- joint author.   II. Title.
[DNLM: 1. Personality development   2. Mental disorders.   3. Interpersonal
relations.   4. Mental disorders—Therapy.   WM100 C466h]
RC506.C46   157   80-13866
ISBN 0-87630-236-3

Published by
BRUNNER/MAZEL, INC.
19 Union Square
New York, New York 10003

NOV 12 81

For

Daisy Belle Appleby Chapman

and for

Miriam K. Dasey

Late Registrar, Yale University School of Medicine

Preface

Harry Stack Sullivan is now generally regarded as the most original, creative American-born psychiatrist. He is the only American psychiatrist to develop an entirely new way of viewing psychiatric illnesses and of treating emotionally disturbed people. His influence on the American mental health professions has been marked, and his viewpoints are gradually reaching a worldwide audience. Sullivan was more of a legend than a well understand person during his lifetime, but his ideas and treatment methods have slowly spread since his death in 1949.

Sullivan discards most previous ideas about personality development and psychiatric disorders, and constructs his concepts on *interpersonal relationships*. This study of *observable things* that go on between people puts psychiatry and other mental health fields on a verifiable scientific basis. Sullivan rejects speculations which cannot be subjected to repeatable observations made by reasonably trained persons. Herein lies the truly revolutionary quality of his thinking and his *interpersonal approach to psychiatry and its allied disciplines*.

The first half of this book traces the evolution of personality from infancy to adulthood. It discusses both normal personality development and abnormal personality development. Sullivan gives detailed attention to the ways in which a personality is molded by an individual's

vii

relationships with the close people in his life and also by interpersonal forces in wider situations.

Discussion of personality development leads naturally to consideration of psychiatric illness. The second half of this book thus presents Sullivan's views on the causes and treatment of various psychiatric disorders. He gives particular attention to anxiety and panic states, obsessive-compulsive disorders, schizophrenia, paranoid conditions, hysterical disturbances, hypochondriacal disorders and various kinds of character malformations.

The material of this book comes from various sources. It depends heavily, of course, on the lectures and seminars which were recorded during the last six years of Sullivan's life and were published in book form in the decade following his death. It also draws on the relatively small number of articles that he wrote in his final years. Sullivan never published a book; the only material of his that appeared in book form while he was alive consisted of five lectures which, against his inclinations, were privately printed and distributed. No distinguished psychiatric pioneer did less to build a monument to himself than Sullivan, and the survival and diffusion of his ideas are a remarkable tribute to their vitality and usefulness.

This book also uses material which we have been collecting on Sullivan since 1948. This includes notes taken by persons who attended his lectures and seminars, unpublished transcripts of recorded teaching sessions, a small amount of material which Sullivan prepared for publication but never printed, and other data. For reasons pointed out in our books, *Harry Stack Sullivan: His Life and His Work* and *The Treatment Techniques of Harry Stack Sullivan,* any valid consideration of Sullivan's ideas must be based on his viewpoints during the last several years of his life. Sullivan spent a long time maturing, both as a person and as a psychiatrist, and only the material of his last five or six years can be accepted as his definitive formulations. He so extensively revised earlier opinions that they can be regarded only as preliminary versions of his final ideas.

Throughout this book we have periodically noted how Sullivan's concepts and techniques of therapy are logical extensions of his views on personality development. We also have inserted brief sections on the therapy of most of the psychiatric disorders discussed. This is done not so much to give instruction on Sullivan's therapeutic methods as to indicate that his views on personality development, psychiatric disorders and treatment form a closely knit whole.

A. H. CHAPMAN
MIRIAM C. M. S. CHAPMAN

Contents

HARRY STACK SULLIVAN'S CONCEPTS OF PERSONALITY DEVELOPMENT AND PSYCHIATRIC ILLNESS

I

SULLIVAN'S CONCEPTS OF PERSONALITY DEVELOPMENT AND THEIR IMPLICATIONS FOR THERAPY

Sullivan divides personality development into four main periods:

1. *Infancy,* which extends from birth to the development of articulate speech as an interpersonal tool.

2. *Childhood,* which begins with the development of articulate speech and ends when the child feels a marked need for relationships with other children.

3. *The juvenile period,* which starts when the person acquires a need for close associations with *nonfamily* children and terminates when sexual maturation begins to exert strong effects on the individual's interpersonal life. Sullivan sometimes separates the last year or so of the juvenile period off as a separate stage which he terms *preadolescence;* however, in this book preadolescence is considered as the terminal phase of the juvenile period.

4. *Adolescence,* which begins when sexual maturation starts to affect interpersonal life and continues until the individual accepts the social, vocational and economic activities considered characteristic of adulthood. Sullivan subdivides adolescence into *early adolescence* and *late adolescence;* this distinction is maintained in this book, though both periods are discussed in the same chapter.

3

Two aspects of this scheme of personality development are note-worthy.

First, the various periods are divided by *interpersonal* features. Thus, articulate speech is viewed as an interpersonal development which opens up new areas, and sexual maturation is seen as a process which has marked effects on the individual's interactions with people. The interpersonal nature of other dividing factors, such as the development of a need for close associations with nonfamily children, is obvious.

Second, exact ages, such as two years or seven years of age, are not used in defining when one period ends and another begins, since individuals vary much in their development of interpersonal needs and abilities. For the sake of clearness, representative age brackets will be mentioned at times in this book, but the numbers are ours, not Sullivan's.

Chapter 1

Infancy

In the first weeks of life an infant's experience consists of a seamless blur of sensations; the infant has no sense of time or space or of himself as something separate from his environment. He also has no sense of the relatedness of things; nothing has clear connections, or separations, from anything else. Sullivan occasionally terms this the prototaxic mode of experience, from the Greek roots indicating, roughly, the first order of things. In later life a person returns to this mode of experience only in some phenomena of sleep, such as in dreams and nightmares, in panic states and in a few kinds of psychiatric illness.

The nature of prototaxic experience may be illustrated in the following manner. An infant feels an indistinct, placeless tension which in later years he will call hunger. He cries. Something is put into his mouth, and in unclear ways his discomfort ceases and he feels at ease. Vague shadows and lights pass before him and hazy pressures are felt on his face, lips and body. He does not connect these sensations in any way, nor divide them into separate experiences. His body, the food, the person caring for him and all things in his environment which cause light, shadows, sounds and pressures form one unpatterned fabric for the infant. It would be incorrect to talk of a flow of events or

5

experiences, since this would imply senses of time and sequence which the infant lacks.

The prototaxic phase of experience, which in its pure form may last only a few weeks, is the only period in the person's life *which is not interpersonal*. Other people, as such, do not exist in it, from the infant's viewpoint. Once the infant has begun to carve out even the faintest concepts of himself and other people, all his subsequent experiences are, in major or minor ways, *interpersonal*. Once he has grasped that he is something distinct from his environment and that there are similar beings hazily present around him, all his experiences are colored by this discovery. Even in such chaotic experiences as dreams, panic states and schizophrenic illnesses, the existence of other people exercises a marked influence on his feelings and ideas. Though in these conditions he may return to the prototaxic mode of living, he is never free of the strong impacts that people have made on him.

After the first few months of life, the most important things in an individual's existence consist of interactions which are going on, have gone on and may in the future go on between him or her and other persons. Life becomes predominantly interpersonal.

The urgent physical needs of the infant propel him into interpersonal development. He or she requires food, water, appropriate clothes and coverings for the maintenance of body temperature. He needs freedom of movement and cleansing of feces and urine. He also has interpersonal requirements. He needs tender, affectionate handling by people who value him or her as a person. These are the first of a long series of *interpersonal necessities* which must be met if he is to develop into an individual who will be able to live comfortably in the complex society he will encounter.

To get these things the infant has only two communicatory tools. He or she can 1) cry, and he or she can 2) subside into relaxed satisfaction when his or her needs are met. He thus communicates before he knows what communication is; he behaves interpersonally before he knows that interpersonal relationships exist. He sets up an interchange of information, sufficient for his needs at the time, between himself and those around him.

THE INCREASINGLY INTERPERSONAL NATURE OF THE INFANT'S EXPERIENCE

Sullivan feels that only *interpersonal* experience can be subjected to scientific study; a person can investigate only those kinds of experiences which can be directly observed between people. All other kinds of experience, such as that which is said to occur in a person's *mind,* or is said to be *intrapsychic,* are beyond the reach of truly scientific study and must forever remain speculative. Many statements may be made about what is going on in a person's mind or is occurring intrapsychically, but since such things can never be observed or otherwise demonstrated, they must always be beyond the reach of proof or disproof.

For example, if a hungry infant cries and his mother gives him food, with subsequent relaxation by the infant and tender acts by the mother, a mental health professional worker can *observe* these events. Much information about this interpersonal incident can be obtained by talking with the mother, by making physiological studies of the child, by making an audiovisual recording and by many other devices. However, if we say that in this experience (to use a Jungian example) the child is achieving the first gratifications of his need to develop his archetype of the All-Giving, or Great, Mother, we are talking about something which is beyond *interpersonal* investigation since it is occurring primarily in the infant's *mind,* or is happening *intrapsychically.* There is no way of observing an archetype; archetypes and all other things said to be lodged in the mind are so postulated that they can be neither proved nor disproved. Statements about them must forever remain conjectures since they are not interpersonally observable nor in any other way demonstrable. Such statements may *explain* a good deal, and much data may be gathered to *corroborate* them. However, an indefinitely large number of quite different statements may *explain* the same events, and they also are beyond the reach of proof or disproof.

This principle forms the basis of all Sullivan's psychology and psychiatry. It separates Sullivan's views on personality development and psychiatric illness from those of all other psychiatric schools of thought.

If any statement in psychology and psychiatry is to be accepted as valid, it must be susceptible to direct confirmation by observing events that occur between two or more people. The alternative is to wander into fields *of unprovable speculation* in which an indefinitely large number of competing schools of psychiatry can grow.

Thus, the actions of an infant have significance *in terms of their interpersonal consequences.* A cry has meaning because the infant is crying for food, or warmth, or cuddling, and this necessity requires *interpersonal* activity; the cry has value and sense for the infant (crude and indistinct though they may be) only when it leads to an interpersonal incident. This is the material that *experience* is made of.

A central feature of an infant's experience is his powerlessness. He has no way of influencing what happens to him, except by crying when uncomfortable and relaxing when satisfied. His major way of losing this helplessness is to slowly acquire the use of symbols in late infancy, childhood and beyond. The acquisition of symbols, the most prominent of which are words and gestures, gradually increases his ability to meet his needs and to modify his environment. Sullivan was the only distinguished psychiatric pioneer in the first half of this century to emphasize the importance of symbols in interpersonal relationships and personality development. *Symbols expand experience.* However, by the connotations a person gives some symbols, such as the words "love" and "bad," they also may limit and distort experience.

All symbols are interpersonal in origin, and they are to a large extent interpersonal in usage. For example, the infant will learn much later that the hairy creature which licks his feet is by common consent a "dog." His mastery of this enables him to ask someone to bring the dog to him or to take it away. Also, once he has *interpersonally* learned to use the symbol "dog," he can think more clearly about the dog when it is not present. Although this is valuable for him, the interpersonal use of this word symbol is even more important as he tries to cope with an increasingly complex world.

Almost all interpersonal life demands the usage of symbols. Even the most primitive kinds of activities with people require the employment of gestures, facial expressions, wordless vocal noises and many kinds of even subtler symbolic communication.

The word symbol has, for many mental health professional workers, a cold, mechanical ring. It smacks of road signs. Sullivan utilizes the term in broader, more vibrant ways. The expression, to oneself and others, of tenseness, hostility, guilt, depressiveness and the whole range of human feelings and experience is impossible without using symbols of some kind. The acquisition of symbols and the refinement of interpersonal relationships go hand in hand, and the process begins in middle infancy.

Overt and Covert Processes. Sullivan draws a distinction between information which is obtained by *overt* methods and that which is obtained by *covert* means. When a psychiatrist or other mental health professional worker can explore some aspect of a patient's experience in a dialogue with him, this information is elicited by an *overt* process. Overt data involve the processes of *participant observation* and *consensual validation,* which we shall discuss in later chapters. However, when information about interpersonal events cannot be acquired in a dialogue, and cannot be validated by exploring it from many points of view with the patient, it is *covert.*

Most of the data on interpersonal relationships we have so far discussed are covert. They are obtained by diligent observation of infants in their interactions with their mothers and other persons. The fact that such information is covert does not make it less useful, so long as we describe how we got the information and recognize its limitations. Any adequately trained observer can confirm it by studying infants and their interactions with the people about them. At some point in the second or third year of life, interpersonal processes become overt; we can begin to get information from the child by the use of words, gestures, shared play and other means.

Overt and *covert* should not be confused with *conscious* and *unconscious;* Sullivan does not use these concepts. Overt and covert do not indicate the nature of the data; they merely indicate how they are obtained. Sullivan accepts many kinds of information, but he insists that the investigator spell out 1) how he got it, 2) why he thinks it is valid,

and 3) how any reasonably trained investigator can verify it in repeatable, objective ways. He feels that failure to do these things has
led many psychiatric systems into sloppy thinking.

THE INFANT'S FIRST CONCEPTS OF OBJECTS

After a few weeks, an infant begins to cleave out of the hazy mass of
his sensations a dim concept of the thing by which he gets his food—
the nipple. It becomes associated in a vague but emotionally powerful
manner with his most urgent need, his satisfaction of hunger. In time
the infant starts to perceive that the nipple is separate from himself.
This is his first crude awareness that the world is divided into two parts
—himself and everything else.

The nipple brings with it the infant's first awareness of sequence.
He senses that a vague but urgent discomfort is followed by crying, and
this in time produces a nipple and satisfaction of hunger. This is his
first glimmering of the *relatedness of things;* he becomes aware that in
the timeless, spaceless chaos—which has so far constituted his experience—certain things are connected to each other in fairly predictable
ways.

The gradual discernment of the nipple leads to the infant's earliest
knowledge of space. The nipple can be absent or present; it can be
approaching or going away. His first perceptions are tactile; he feels
the nipple in his mouth. He later correlates certain patterns of light
and shadow, and sensations of sound, taste and smell, with the appearance and withdrawal of the nipple.

In a similar manner the infant begins to get a cloudy sense of time.
Hunger, crying and the nipple come in predictable sequences and at
varying rates of speed. As a sense of time commences, it brings with it
flickerings of recall and foresight. This is the start of the concepts he
much later will call the past, the present and the future.

All these developments, sometimes lumped together under the term
*cognitive, are from the psychiatric point of view much overshadowed
by the emotional factors connected with them.*

At times the mother, or whoever else is feeding the infant, presents the nipple to him in a relaxed, affectionate manner, and from these experiences he gradually acquires a set of feelings and primitive thoughts which Sullivan groups together under the term *the good,* or *emotionally comfortable, nipple.*

At other times the mother, or other person caring for the child, gives him the nipple in a cold, irritable or tense manner, and the infant at these times is flooded with feelings of apprehensiveness and other forms of emotional pain. Out of many experiences of this kind the child develops in time a set of feelings, attitudes and primitive thoughts to which Sullivan gives the name *the bad,* or *anxiety-producing, nipple.*

In the infant's first faint perceptions, there are thus two nipples; one is emotionally comfortable, or good, and the other is anxiety-producing, or bad. *This is the child's first awareness that all his experiences throughout his life will fall into one of two broad categories. They will be either emotionally comfortable or emotionally painful. They will be either anxiety-free or anxiety-laden.*

At this point Sullivan's definition of the term anxiety must be made clear. He employs the word in a much broader manner than many other psychiatric writers do. *Anxiety includes all forms of emotional pain; it embraces tension, apprehensiveness, panic, guilt, shame, self-loathing, self-depreciation, eerie awe and all other types of emotional distress.* In Sullivan's psychology and psychiatry, the terms anxiety and emotional pain are synonymous.

Such a broad use of the word *anxiety* may at first seem strange to mental health professional workers who are accustomed to its employment in much more restricted ways. Sullivan feels, however, that the fragmentation of emotional pain into several neat categories is unsound and arbitrary. He feels that a mental health professional worker will become convinced of this if he notes his own feelings when he is truly upset; he will find that neat division and labeling of his turmoil can be done only by oversimplifying his distress.

To recapitulate, the infant's first urgent interpersonal relationships are with the persons who in many kinds of emotional atmospheres feed him. In these interpersonal incidents the infant has his first experiences with emotional comfort and emotional pain, or anxiety. Out of them the infant forms two groups of feelings, attitudes and primitive ideas—the emotionally comfortable, or good, nipple and the anxiety-producing, or bad, nipple.

THE INTERPERSONAL SIGNIFICANCE OF THE INFANT'S FIRST CONCEPTS OF OBJECTS

In the final phase of infancy and during early childhood, the two concepts of the emotionally comfortable (good) nipple and the anxiety-producing (bad) nipple are fused into a single conception of *nipple*. This conception of the nipple embodies both comfortable and painful features, and their relative proportions have marked effects on the person's view of the world about him. If the bulk of his interpersonal experiences in feeding and other person-to-person activities have been emotionally comfortable, and if few of these experiences have been contaminated with emotional pain, he will tend to view the world as a secure, reassuring place. If, on the other hand, the majority of his feeding experiences and other interpersonal contacts have been tainted with hostility, rejection and other forms of emotional distress, he will tend to view the world as a painful, threatening place.

These early impressions of the world can be much modified in both healthy and unhealthy ways by subsequent experiences in childhood, adolescence and adulthood. However, the events of infancy have special force since they are molding a person who has had no previous experience. They are, so to speak, inscribing their marks on a chalkboard which is blank; the experiences of later years make their imprints on a chalkboard which has already been extensively engraved with designs.

Other objects besides the nipple have, of course, effects on the infant. The clothing that keeps him warm, the fresh diapers that keep him dry, the lukewarm water that cleans him and many other things slowly become distinct. The interpersonal comfort or discomfort which he feels as he is clothed, or diapered or washed by persons who are affectionate or hostile all contribute to his perception of the world as inviting or menacing. Thus, it would be possible to talk about emotionally comfortable (good) and anxiety-laden (bad) bathing experiences, in the same way that we talk about good and bad nipple experiences. The same general principle could be applied to all objects *involved in interpersonal relationships* between the infant and the persons caring for him.

However, no experience of the infant has the emotional impact of feeding. Hunger is the most urgent discomfort the infant has, and it occurs frequently. Food is his most acute need, and getting it requires much interpersonal activity. Keeping clean, staying warm and similar things do not have the pressing force of hunger, and the interpersonal acts to attend to these needs are usually brief and simple, in comparison with feeding.

Moreover, feeding is concentrated on an area of the body, the mouth and adjacent regions, that has a particularly rich innervation; it is sensuous. Wherever skin meets a mucous membrane, as in the mouth, anus and genitals, the number of nerve endings is much greater than in areas of skin or mucous membrane alone, and in some regions there also are special nerve receptors whose stimulation gives exceptional gratification or distress. Interpersonal experiences which are concentrated on a skin-mucous membrane junction, as in feeding, therefore have large emotional charges. For this added reason, the contact of the nipple with the lips has more effect on an infant than the application of clothes to his body and similar activities.

Furthermore, the infant usually experiences the same favorable or unfavorable attitudes from his mother or other person taking care of him during bathing, diapering and kindred events; the mother who is irritable, or frightened or depressed when she is feeding the child probably feels similarly when doing other things with him. In a sense, the terms emotionally comfortable (good) nipple and anxiety-producing (bad) nipple encompass a broad range of *interpersonal experiences* in which material objects are involved.

Sullivan stresses that such things as the emotionally comfortable (good) nipple and the anxiety-producing (bad) nipple do not exist in the sense that bushes and trees exist. These terms are merely literary conveniences which we use to designate broad groups of feelings and primitive thoughts in the infant. These expressions simply allow us to talk concisely about the complex things the infant is experiencing.

This is a crucial point in Sullivan's psychology and psychiatry. It also is a thing which mental health professional workers trained in other psychiatric schools frequently have difficulty in grasping. Sullivan insists that things like a Jungian archetype or a Freudian ego or super-ego are merely literary conveniences, or metaphors. The distinguished Austrian-British philosopher of science, Sir Karl Popper, who increasingly is recognized as the most important authority on the logic of science since Francis Bacon, has gone so far as to say that such Jungian and Freudian concepts as archetypes and superegos can only be considered mythologies.

Thus, such things as the emotionally comfortable (good) nipple and the anxiety-producing (bad) nipple, do not exist in patients; they exist only in the minds of psychiatrists and other mental health professional workers who are thinking and talking about patients and need word formulas to help them to do so. The patients have only their satisfactions, terrors, passions and thoughts.

Sullivan stresses that if a mental health professional worker mistakenly believes that things like archetypes and egos exist as actual objects, and if he begins to manipulate and subdivide them in elaborate ways, he has abandoned hope of ever establishing his viewpoints on sound scientific bases.

Sullivan avoids such errors by recognizing the true nature of the terms he is employing to talk about human comfort and suffering.

THE INFANT'S FIRST CONCEPTS OF PERSONS

Out of his daily contacts with his mother, or other person caring for him, an infant slowly evolves his first concept of a person. He gradually grasps that there is a physical being who is doing things with him, and in a crude manner he clutches at his first interpersonal relationship. The nature of this relationship has a marked influence on him.

In the interactions with his mother in which she is affectionate and relaxed, the infant in time develops the concept of an *emotionally comfortable mother;* Sullivan calls this, for brevity's sake, the *good mother.*

Out of those experiences in which the mother, or one of her substitutes, is tense, irritable and rejecting, the infant evolves the concept of the *anxiety-producing mother;* Sullivan employs the term *bad mother* to designate concisely this group of uncomfortable feelings and primitive thoughts in the infant.

The mother's affection, or apprehensiveness, or hostility is perceived empathically by the infant by the ways in which she handles him, in her vocal tones and in similar things. The word empathy, as used here, indicates a wide range of mainly nonverbal ways in which feelings and attitudes are conveyed from one person to another; Sullivan, somewhat graphically, occasionally calls this process "emotional contagiousness."

In his first interpersonal relationship an infant thus develops a broad division which will last all his life and will characterize all his relationships with people. His relationships with people will be either emotionally comfortable (good) or anxiety-producing (bad). Of course, it is rare that an interpersonal relationship is purely comfortable or painful; each relationship is a mixture of both features.

Whether an interpersonal relationship at any time in a person's life is *healthy* or *unhealthy* depends on whether the comfortable or anxiety-laden factors dominate. Using the artificial but convenient terminology of percentages, we may say that, if a relationship is 90 percent comfortable and 10 percent anxious, it is a gratifying association and probably is healthy. If, in contrast, a relationship is 50 percent comfortable and 50 percent painful, it is stressful. If it is 90 percent anxiety-ridden and 10 percent comfortable, it is an anguished relationship and probably a sick one. An individual's psychological health at any point in his life is similarly determined; if most of his relationships with people are reasonably comfortable, he probably is emotionally healthy, but if most of them are disturbed by emotional turmoil, he in most cases is sick.

Sullivan employs the word *tenderness,* almost as a technical term, in discussing what goes on in the mother-child relationship. *Tenderness* designates all the affectionate, anxiety-free things that go on between the mother and the child. It does not exist solely in the mother or in the child, but *interpersonally* embraces the things that go on between the two of them. The stimuli which set tenderness in operation are the physiological needs of the infant and his powerlessness to meet any of them. These needs elicit affectionate, anxiety-free attention by the mother. Tenderness, an interpersonal process, is present when the needs of the child and the anxiety-free care of the mother interweave harmoniously. *The degree to which tenderness is present, or is defective or distorted, determines how the child's concepts of the emotionally comfortable (good) mother and the anxiety-producing (bad) mother are developed.*

LONG-TERM EFFECTS OF THE INFANT'S EARLIEST CONCEPTS OF PERSONS

For almost one-third of his life an individual in our culture is at least partially dependent on his parents and other caring and educating people who slowly mold him into a human being. As has been pointed out above in somewhat different terms, psychiatric health or sickness is determined by whether things go well or badly in the multiple interpersonal relationships which the person has as he or she proceeds from the complete helplessness of infancy through the periods of partial dependence which come afterwards.

In these pages we are employing the word mother as a collective term to cover all persons who participate to an appreciable extent in the care of the infant. Sullivan uses terms such as "the mothering one," "mother surrogates" and others to transmit this concept. The infant's father, older siblings, and other persons who care for him thus enter into his concepts of the emotionally comfortable and anxiety-producing mother. In his early months an infant cannot distinguish one person from another; knowing people as distinct individuals comes only in middle and late infancy. Indeed, the expressions emotionally comfortable (good) *person* and anxiety-producing (bad) *person* might in many cases be substituted for the equivalent terms employing the word *mother*.

In the second year of life the infant begins to formulate his experiences in words. *At this time he fuses the emotionally comfortable mother and the anxiety-producing mother into a single concept of mother.* Encapsulated in this concept, both the emotionally comfortable and anxiety-producing mothers continue to be present. Depending on their relative proportions and the ways in which they are interwoven, the child looks upon mothers, and interpersonal relationships in general, as predominantly comfortable or painful, or as complex mixtures of both. Whether, throughout childhood, adolescence and adulthood, a person views associations with people as inviting or threatening, or a blend of both these qualities, is much influenced by this first, powerful impression. However, as we shall discuss in later chapters, a person's interpersonal capacities may be much improved or worsened by what happens in subsequent epochs of his life.

Nipple concepts are developed mainly by the sense of touch in direct physical contact with the nipple and the person giving it, whereas mother concepts require extensive use of distance sensory perceptions such as seeing and hearing. This, combined with the fact that *persons* are much more complex than *things,* causes mother concepts to be developed later than nipple concepts. Moreover, in developing mother, or person, concepts, the child's grasp of time, space and other cognitive functions becomes tied to interpersonal relationships. From this point forward, the child will think and feel about time and space (places) in terms of their connections with people; as he gradually develops his ideas about the past, the present and the future he will tie them to what they mean in terms of what happened, is happening and will happen between him and other persons.

A note on Sullivan's terminology is advisable at this point to orient readers who may go on to read his works. He employs the term *personification* to designate such things as the emotionally comfortable (good) mother and the anxiety-producing (bad) mother, as well as others which we shall discuss in the next section of this chapter. In place of the somewhat cumbersome word *personification,* the term *concept* is utilized in this book. It is easier to talk about an infant's concept of the emotionally comfortable mother than his personification of her. As dealt with in our book *Harry Stack Sullivan: His Life and His Work,* Sullivan's atypical education caused him at times to utilize words which have confused his readers and retarded the spread of his viewpoints.

THE INFANT'S CONCEPTS OF HIMSELF

In the same way that he develops nipple (object) and mother (person) concepts, an infant slowly develops concepts of himself.

In those contacts with his mother and others in which he is treated with affection and esteem, he gradually acquires a concept of *the emotionally comfortable (good) me*. This concept embraces feelings of himself as a worthwhile, valuable, esteemed person. Simultaneously with the formation of the concept of the emotionally comfortable (good) me, the infant generates the concept of *the anxiety-ridden me,* which Sullivan as a rule refers to as *the bad me*. Each experience in which he is treated with irritability, depreciation, rejection and other damaging feelings contributes to the conception of himself as a worthless, unloved, incapable individual. Feelings and ideas of personal inadequacy, self-loathing, interpersonal ineptness and other kinds of emotional distress are encapsulated in *the anxiety-ridden (bad) me*.

In addition, the infant forms a third concept of himself. In interactions with persons who are crudely rejecting, or emotionally brutal or panicky with him, he in time evolves the concept of *the panic-ridden me,* which Sullivan often terms the *not-me*. The feelings of panic, chaos, profound self-loathing and eerie dread which are encapsulated in the panic-ridden (not) me are beyond clear expression in words. When in later years a person has become skillful with language, he as a rule can express some components of the emotionally comfortable (good) me, the anxiety-producing (bad) mother and similar concepts we have discussed. However, the feelings of terror, self-abhorrence and uncanny horror which are encased in the panic-ridden (not) me are beyond formulation in words. In later life the panic-ridden me is manifest only in panic states, acute schizophrenic disorders and other states of personality disintegration.

Toward the end of infancy and in early childhood, the infant's three concepts of himself are welded into one. Language facilitates the process of merging these concepts into "I," "myself" and other self-referring terms. A person's overall conception of himself, and his feelings about himself as an interpersonal being, are determined by the

the interpersonal nature and causes of his emotional distress; he senses only that he is flooded with emotional pain. Sullivan feels that the anxiety of infancy is probably the most intense anxiety a person has at any time in his life. Hence, he feels that all later anxiety harkens back to the anxiety the person felt in infancy; it is the suffering upon which all later experiences of anxiety are based.

THE INTERPERSONAL CONSEQUENCES OF AN INFANT'S ANXIETY

Although there is nothing *specific* the infant can do to decrease his anxiety, his *nonspecific* crying may be interpersonally important. His crying may cause his mother to take stock of what is going on between her and her child, and as a result she may relax and give him the affectionate care he needs. This happens mainly when the mother's tension is minor and brief, and probably occurs a great deal in healthy mother-child situations. The infant's crying acts as a regulator that keeps the mother-child relationship on a sound course most of the time.

In some cases, however, crying worsens the mother-child relationship. An anxiety-ridden, crying child makes his mother more apprehensive, or insecure, or depressed, and the mother's mounting turmoil augments the child's anxiety, creating a vicious circle. Emotional tension in infants can produce in them eating problems, fitful sleep, digestive difficulties and other dysfunctions, and these may further increase the mother's unhealthy feelings toward the child; they may cause the mother to feel that her unfavorable attitudes toward this "difficult" or "unresponsive" child are justified.

From late infancy onward, foresight contributes to anxiety. For example, the infant who has experienced discomfort in large numbers of feeding incidents may dread each approaching feeding. His anxiety begins when hunger warns him that once more a tension-filled contact with his mother is near. *Anxiety thus precedes the interpersonal event.* Foresight, as a cause of anxiety, is crude and limited in infants; it becomes elaborate and complex in children, adolescents and adults.

This is an example of a process to which we shall give more attention in later chapters. *Anxiety frequently obstructs the interpersonal relationships which might solve it.* An anxiety-laden person is crippled to some extent in his abilities to deal with the interpersonal situations which are causing his anxiety. An anxious marital partner, whose emotional turmoil is to a marked degree caused by his difficulties with his mate, is hindered by his anxiety in talking out his problems with his spouse or in resolving their problems in other ways. Hence, *anxiety is both a result of interpersonal difficulties and a cause of prolonging and worsening them.*

Anxiety in an infant can be reduced only by changes in the feelings and actions of the mother and other persons caring for the child. By intuition (guided more by feelings than by articulate awareness) or by deliberate action, the mother must begin to give the child relaxed, sensitive care. A mother who has a reasonably sound personality, and who is not caught up in ongoing interpersonal turbulence in some segment of her life (such as a marital crisis), can do this. A mother whose ingrained personality difficulties prevent her from doing this, or whose interpersonal life keeps her in chronic turmoil, often cannot do so without professional help.

The opposite of anxiety is *security.* Security is a state of relaxed comfort in which the individual has a firm sense of his worth and adeptness as a person; he has good capacities for dealing with people in a wide range of situations. *All interpersonal relationships are directed, in small or large ways, toward achieving security and avoiding anxiety.* Security and anxiety may be somewhat roughly imagined as being on the opposite ends of a seesaw; they are always in a fluctuating balance with each other.

In every interpersonal relationship there is an *anxiety gradient.* The term anxiety gradient designates the degrees of emotional comfort, or security, and emotional discomfort, or anxiety, at any particular time. Each person constantly modifies his acts and attitudes to remain secure and to avoid anxiety. The amounts of anxiety which most people deal with most of the time are small; often they are trivial. In addition, most of the time a person is unaware of his degree of anxiety; that is, his anxiety gradient lies outside his focus of awareness. He makes his interpersonal adjustments in his characteristic ways for remaining comfortable, and gives no articulate attention to how he does this. At other times the anxiety gradient brings emotional pain into his focus of awareness, and he may do many kinds of things to return to a more comfortable state. The sorts of things a person does, in both healthy and unhealthy ways, to shift his anxiety gradient back toward comfort will occupy much of our attention in later chapters.

The anxiety gradient is a major force in governing human behavior. In infancy its functioning is crude and erratic; in childhood, adolescence and adulthood the anxiety gradient's operations are refined. Though the anxiety gradient does not produce interpersonal relationships, it plays a strong role in determining what happens in them. The anxiety gradient and its vicissitudes are responsible for many kinds of symptoms and interpersonal maladjustments that come to the attention of mental health professional workers.

NEEDS AND INTERPERSONAL INTEGRATIONS

In the first two decades of life, a skillful animal is gradually molded into a human being. Interpersonal relationships cause this evolution; interpersonal relationships, in turn, are created by the person's needs. Sullivan employs the word *need* as a technical term. It indicates a biological or interpersonal necessity which must be met if an individual is to be physically at ease and to have adequate self-esteem and security.

Needs cause interpersonal integrations; each need moves a person into one or more interpersonal associations in which the need can be satisfied. In the simplest of examples, the infant's need for food causes him to cry, and this *integrates* him with his mother. In later years a person's needs tend to be interpersonal rather than physical; however, the hallmark of a need remains its stimulus to integrate a person in an interpersonal relationship. In later chapters we shall discuss the dominant needs in each epoch of life (infancy, childhood, the juvenile period and others) and outline the main kinds of interpersonal integrations they cause.

Emotional problems arise when a person's needs are met in unhealthy ways. For example, if an infant receives attention from a rejecting mother only when he goes into a howling rage, or from an apprehensive mother only when he refuses food, his needs are being met in unhealthy ways and are contributing to sick interpersonal relationships. Multiple, prolonged disturbances of these kinds lead to personality malformations. In contrast, when a need is met in a healthy way, a sound integration occurs; the individual then seeks to resolve his need in the same manner the next time the need arises, whether that need be food for an infant, sexual urges in an adolescent or companionship in persons of older age groups.

To recapitulate, anxiety breeds anxiety and blocks the satisfaction of needs. The rejecting mother floods her child with inarticulate dread and the hostile marital partner produces insecurity or revulsion in his spouse. In each instance, the person's basic needs are not being met; they remain goading sources of suffering and often drive the person to seek satisfactions in ways that are unhealthy. On a larger scale, whether people's needs are met in healthy or unhealthy ways determines whether family groups, work teams and other social groups are sound or sick. To a large extent, these things form the field with which psychiatry concerns itself.

THE WEB OF INTERPERSONAL RELATIONSHIPS
SURROUNDING THE INFANT

The personality evolution of an infant is affected, in addition, by the network of interpersonal relationships that stretches out from him on all sides. If his mother was embroiled in a sick relationship with her own mother, his needs are unlikely to be met. If he is born into a fear-ridden inner city district, he has little chance of having his physical and interpersonal needs satisfied in esteem-building ways. If his parents are chronically grounded by economic difficulties, they may be unable to give him the affection and security his personality development requires.

Sullivan was the first distinguished psychiatric pioneer to stress the impacts of such far-reaching interpersonal webs on personality development during infancy and beyond. As early as the 1920s he emphasized that the basic problems of many sick people were to a large extent produced by the unhealthy society he saw around him, and he stressed this from the viewpoint of clinical psychiatry.

Sullivan employs the somewhat cryptic phrase "illusion of personal individuality" to indicate that an individual has significance and meaning only in the context of his relationships with other people. An individual at no time lives in an interpersonal vacuum; *all his personality characteristics at any moment are, in the final analysis, defined in terms of his relationships with people.* If we say that Mary is passive and that John is aggressive, we are really saying that Mary is passive *in her associations with others* and that John is aggressive *in his dealings with people.* It makes no sense to visualize Mary or John divorced from the interpersonal worlds in which they live.

Moreover, the fact that we can make statements about Mary's passivity or John's aggressiveness is based on our first having formed interpersonal relationships with them in order to evaluate each one. Even such a seemingly self-contained thing as intelligence is understandable only in terms of interpersonal associations. For example, to say that Nancy has superior intelligence makes sense only by comparing her with others, and we can say that Charles is retarded only in the context of what many other people of his age and cultural background can do. Put in other terms, the idea that we can say anything about anyone's personality, except in terms of his past and present interpersonal relationships, is an illusion.

The crucial, even revolutionary, importance of Sullivan's concept of the illusion of personal individuality lies in what it says about the concept of *mind,* a subject we looked at from a different angle in Chapter 1. Sullivan rejects the concept of *mind* in psychology and psychiatry, for once such a concept is accepted anyone can describe its contents in any manner he chooses, and his statements are neither provable nor disprovable since there is no way of observing the mind in objective scientific ways. In Sullivan's words, anyone can arrange the mind's furniture in any way he wishes. Since no one can demonstrate that his particular arrangement of mental furniture is more valid than anyone else's, the way is open for innumerable schemes about how things in the mind are set up. The result is the interminable proliferation of new schools of psychology and psychiatry, and their acceptance must depend on their proponents' eloquence and ingenuity rather than their ability to contrive objective, repeatable scientific experiments to settle the matter.

The concept of mind *is* acceptable in philosophy, religion and popular belief, since these systems of thought do not require that their statements are capable of proof or disproof. Science demands that the statements can be validated. By basing his approach to psychology and psychiatry on interpersonal relationships (observable things that go on between people), Sullivan is placing himself on scientific ground and is holding out the opportunity for psychiatry to evolve in time into a truly scientific discipline.

Relating these things to infancy, an infant can be understood only in terms of what goes on between him and other people. The personality he begins to develop makes sense only when viewed as the product of all his experiences with people.

INTERPERSONAL COMMUNICATION IN INFANCY

Sullivan considers communication in infancy in terms of *signs, signals* and *symbols*. They develop in roughly that order of sequence, and are of much importance in the evolution of interpersonal life.

At some point in the early weeks of life an infant becomes dimly aware that a howl brings food and the satisfaction of hunger. The howl comes to be a *sign* for him and his mother; it is communicatory, though very crudely so. Out of the blurred mass of his experience, this sign is separated as having special meaning.

This sign slowly evolves into a signal. It is a signal when the infant becomes *aware* that it can produce a fairly *predictable* alteration in the flow of his experience, and that this alteration involves *interpersonal* figures, however vague they may as yet be. The things that distinguish a signal from a sign are the infant's *awareness,* however crude, of the *clear predictability* of its results and its *interpersonal* connotations.

Eventually, signals develop into *symbols,* which we considered in another context in the first chapter. A symbol is a sound, an inscription or some similar device which designates something. The word bread can be spoken, or written, or indicated by the trademark of a bread company, but the word bread cannot be eaten—it is a symbol that designates something that can be eaten. When at the end of infancy the person begins to employ symbols, the use of signs and signals quickly recedes, though to some extent they remain present throughout life. The child's interpersonal life expands at a very fast rate because he can communicate his needs, feelings and experiences in much more forceful ways. This utilization of spoken and written symbols is intertwined with, and exists alongside, an extensive system of nonverbal communication by facial expressions, gestures, body stances and other wordless channels.

AUTISM AND COMMUNICATION

Many of the first words that the child develops are *autistic*. The hallmark of autistic language is that it is *noninterpersonal;* the symbols in it cannot be used to communicate with others.

Thus, the child may utilize the sound "grat" as he struggles to get a word symbol which will enable him to talk with others about the family cat and to think articulately about it. This word, like all his autistic words and symbols, is peculiarly his own; he can share it with no one else. A passage through a phase of autistic thinking occurs in all persons. A few children develop extensive autistic languages, but they soon discard them. Most children go through their autistic period in a helter-skelter way in the final phase of infancy and during early childhood. They develop various autistic words and phrases and then discard them as the generally accepted word symbols are mastered.

Autistic language does not "disappear," however. Like all other things in a person's life, it becomes part of his total experience. An individual may return to this autistic mode of thinking and talking in dreams, panic states, schizophrenic illnesses and other states of primitive or deteriorated personality functioning. As will be unfolded in later chapters, all the things we are discussing in personality development are closely connected with Sullivan's concepts of psychiatric illness.

Sullivan's emphasizes that *symbols exist in the person*. The "grat" exists only inside the head of the child; it does not exist in the cat or anywhere else "out there." It, moreover, becomes manifest only in an interpersonal relationship; we cannot know that the sound, or symbol, "grat" exists until the child tells somebody about it while attempting to talk about the cat. Later the child masters the word "cat" and discards use of "grat." He can now think more clearly about the cat because he can exchange information about its habits and whereabouts with the people around him. The interpersonally correct symbol "cat," which the child later will learn to represent by the letters c-a-t, *now exists in the child*. The most important thing, however, is that it also exists, by common consent, in his parents and others. It is not inherent in the nature of cats, which might be called anything else. The prime importance of symbols is hence manifest; they are arbitrary, artificial conveniences *which make interpersonal relationships richer and easier. They thus help personality grow*.

These artificial conveniences have extensive clinical implications. For example, a schizophrenic, among other things, is a person who, because of interpersonal remoteness, is using symbols which other people don't employ. He thinks and talks of "grats" and not "cats." The difference (in this very restricted sense) between a sick person and a well one is that the sick person employs symbols which are not useful in interpersonal relationships, and the healthy person utilizes symbols which are helpful in interpersonal associations. Schizophrenia is, of course, much more complex than this, but this is a significant aspect of the disorder.

Many symbols become charged with strong feelings and attitudes during infancy and childhood; this happens when they are connected with comfortable or uncomfortable interpersonal experiences. Even a common symbol like the word cat may become emotionally charged in constructive or destructive ways. The child may have feelings of affection, or tension or terror when he thinks about a cat or uses this word in talking with someone. These feelings and attitudes are determined by the kinds of interpersonal experiences the child has had concerning the cat. Did the child and his parents together cuddle the cat, or fight about it, or did the parents flood the child with fears that it might transmit diseases?

The child's feelings and interpersonal associations about such symbols as *mother, father, good, bad, I* and innumerable others are much stronger and much more complex. These symbols also constitute one of the main means by which mental health professional workers try to understand and help upset people, since language is a major tool of therapy. When all these aspects of the word *symbol* are considered, it ceases to have the sterile, mechanical sound it first may have for many mental health professional workers; it is seen as important *in understanding interpersonal relationships, personality growth and the techniques utilized to help sick people.*

Chapter 3

Childhood

Childhood extends from the acquisition of articulate speech to the time at which the child acquires a strong need for associations with nonfamily children of his own age. Though Sullivan assigns no age numbers to the boundaries of childhood, we may, for clarity's sake, put them roughly between one-and-a-half and four years of age.

THE CHILD'S EXPANDING WORLD OF
INTERPERSONAL RELATIONSHIPS

During this period a steadily increasing number of people have impacts on the child. His father, siblings, other members of the extended family and other persons whom he encounters in the home and outside it influence him. Language, in combination with ever greater skill in the nonverbal aspects of communication with people, greatly changes the child's views of people. Persons no longer loom up before him in the vague but powerful forms we have embodied in terms such as the emotionally comfortable (good) mother and kindred personifications. Each person has a name, a face and identifying interpersonal characteristics.

This both simplifies and complicates the child's dealings with people. It is simpler to have each person in his environment neatly categorized as mother, father, Barbara, Bruce and others. However, each of these words hides a wide range of feelings and interpersonal attitudes; the comfortable and anxiety-producing aspects of his interpersonal life no longer are as clear-cut as when he dealt only with the emotionally comfortable (good) mother, the anxiety-producing (bad) mother and others. It is easier to ask "What effect has the anxiety-producing (bad) mother on the child?" than "What is the effect of Barbara on the child?" Language both conceals and clarifies.

The interpersonal relationships of childhood may correct earlier emotional traumas; they also may damage the personality structure of a child whose earlier experiences were sound. For example, a child may improve much if he has sound, esteem-building relationships with his father and an older sibling after an anxiety-producing relationship with his mother in infancy; the healthy later relationships may largely erase the prior traumas. On the other hand, a child may lose some of the sound personality evolution he had during the first year and a half of his life if the experiences of childhood are hostile, depreciating and rejecting. Personality is always flexible. It is always, under the impacts of ongoing interpersonal relationships, changing in healthy or unhealthy directions, and it may be altering for the better in one area while changing for the worse in another.

Sullivan feels that there is a stronger tendency for sound relationships in childhood to erase unfortunate developments in infancy than for untoward relationships in childhood to undermine good personality evolution during infancy. Thus, the child who had good personality growth during infancy tends to withstand emotionally damaging relationships fairly well in childhood, and the child who had harmful relationships in infancy tends to improve if he has a better interpersonal life throughout his childhood years. This is an aspect of Sullivan's principle *the tendency toward health,* which we shall discuss in more detail in Chapter 7.

The tendency toward health principle implies, among other things, that constructive interpersonal experiences generally have more effects on personality growth than destructive ones, regardless of whether the destructive influences come before or after the constructive ones. Thus, healthy influences tend to erase previous unhealthy ones, and early healthy development tends to withstand subsequent interpersonal buffeting. This is only a general trend; the strengths of the involved healthy and unhealthy factors affect the final outcomes in different persons. There is a general inclination for this plasticity of personality to decrease as a person grows older. A person can more readily undergo major changes of personality in childhood and the juvenile period than in late adolescence and adulthood; nevertheless, all individuals retain extensive capacities for personality change all their lives.

THE EVOLUTION OF PERSONALITY

Though we have talked much about personality we have not yet defined it. *Personality consists of the characteristic ways in which an individual deals with people in his interpersonal relationships.* Personality is thus delineated entirely in *interpersonal* terms and is based on things which any reasonably trained observer can see, hear and feel in his interactions with a person. It does not rely on unobservable, speculative things.

If asked to describe the personality of Deborah, age three, an observer after studying her might say that she is at ease in her relationships with her parents, competitive and apprehensive in her relationship with her two-year-old brother and tense in associations with persons whom she does not know well. She is alertly perceptive of what goes on between herself and others and conforms reasonably well to what children and adults in her environment expect of her; however, she can be assertive of her rights. In times of stress she clings, both emotionally and physically, to her parents, but at other times has the kinds of self-reliance and independence that are characteristic of a three-year-old child. This description of Deborah's *personality could be much extended, but each item would relate to some aspect of what goes on between her and other people.*

The uniqueness of Sullivan's *interpersonal definition of personality* is best seen by comparing it with other ways of describing personality. It does not mention Deborah's collective unconscious mind, ego strengths, volitional strivings and hosts of similar things from diverse psychological schools of thought. As noted above, Sullivan objects to all such concepts in discussing personality since they deal with things which defy objective recording and proof.

A central word in Sullivan's definition of personality is *characteristic*. It is the fairly predictable, *characteristic* features of her relationships with people which distinguish Deborah, and these characteristics have a tendency to develop into long-lasting patterns. If she is well adjusted in her interpersonal life at eight and 18, she is likely to be so at 38 and 48. Despite its continual modifications by changing forces in interpersonal life, basic personality trends tend to persist.

THE DEVELOPMENT OF SECURITY OPERATIONS

A security operation is an interpersonal activity or attitude which a person characteristically employs to avoid emotional pain (anxiety) and achieve emotional comfort (security).

As a rule, a person is not aware of his security operations. They are ingrained aspects of his personality functioning which lie outside the scope of his awareness. They begin to develop during childhood.

Security operations should not be confused with things such as Freudian mechanisms of defense, Jungian manifestations of archetypes and similar functions in other psychiatric systems. The fundamental difference is that an operation such as a Freudian mechanism of defense, like repression or introjection, is an unobservable occurrence in the mind of a person; it is an unverifiable conjecture which is designed to explain something the person does, or thinks or feels. In *contrast, a security operation consists of acts, words and attitudes which can be directly observed in interpersonal relationships. The kinds of security operations which a person employs to keep himself in an emotionally comfortable state are characteristic of him; he tends to use them repeatedly in anxiety-producing situations.*

The nature of security operations is illustrated by describing a typical one, which Sullivan calls the *as if* security operation. In it, a person acts in an interpersonal situation *as if* something painful does not exist, or is quite different from its true nature. For example, a child who is locked in a relationship with a cold, domineering mother avoids being aware of the uncomfortable aspects of this relationship by acting *as if* his mother is quite different than she really is. In feelings, thoughts and acts, he behaves with his mother *as if* her coldness is a constructive thing which is helping him to become a self-reliant, independent person, and *as if* her domination of him is guiding him in the development of socially desirable qualities. The true nature of his *as if* security operation lies outside his field of awareness, and with this the child makes his relationship with his mother emotionally endurable; he evades awareness of the painful realities of the situation. This *as if* security operation is unhealthy; in it the child is adjusting to a sick relationship by conforming with its unsound demands.

In time this *as if* security operation becomes an ingrained aspect of the child's interaction with his mother, *and he will tend to carry it into other interpersonal relationships. It will become characteristic of him; he will use similar as if security operations during adolescence and adulthood unless subsequent relationships with people help him to acquire healthier modes of adjustment.*

Security operations may be healthy or unhealthy, and there are many kinds of them. We cannot list and give examples of all these security operations here. We wish merely to indicate that their formation begins in childhood and continues during the juvenile period and much of adolescence.

One security operation, however, is so important that detailed coverage of it is necessary; it is *selective inattention*. In selective inattention, a person, in ways he does not perceive, excludes interpersonally painful things from his field of awareness. The ways in which selective inattention operates is made clear in describing a particular interpersonal situation. A child's father chronically treats him with irritability and rejection. This is too painful for the child to include in his field of awareness, and he *selectively inattends* it—in ways which he does not comprehend, he blots it from his perception. He notes only those acts and attitudes of his father which he can comfortably accept, and does not perceive those aspects of their relationship which would be emotionally devastating to him. By virtue of this security operation, his relationship with his father is tolerable.

Selective inattention is universal. From childhood onward, everyone employs it to some extent all his life in almost all his interpersonal relationships. Whether it is healthy or unhealthy depends on the degree to which it is used and the importance of the particular interpersonal relationship. Thus, if selective inattention is used only to exclude trivial things from awareness, it may be healthy. Most parent-child, marital and other relationships are workable only because each person *selectively inattends* many minor features of another person's acts and attitudes. Difficulties arise when important areas of a relationship are selectively shunted out of awareness; the relationship then becomes unrealistic, or emotionally dangerous, or socially unacceptable for one or both parties.

The hazardous feature of selective inattention is that *the things which are shunted out of the person's focus of attention do not become part of his general body of experience. From the viewpoint of the person, it is as if they never occurred. Since they do not pass through his field of awareness they do not join the fund of experience on which he can draw in forming attitudes and making decisions in subsequent life events.*

Thus, the individual may make the same errors, and repeat the same sick patterns, indefinitely in many kinds of interpersonal settings. For example, in the first of the two cases cited above, during adolescence and adulthood the child may feel that all persons who treat him in cold, domineering ways are helping him to become self-reliant and to develop socially desirable qualities. As a result, he may select a cold, domineering marital partner and allow cold, domineering people to control his social and vocational life; he does these things because in innumerable incidents from childhood onward the security operation of selective inattention has robbed him all his life of the perceived experience which would have helped to lead him into healthier ways of living.

Some kinds of security operations, when they are severe, cause such extensive problems that we say the involved persons are emotionally maladjusted, or psychiatrically ill. Much of the work of psychiatrists and other mental health professionals consists of bringing unhealthy security operations into people's fields of awareness, so they may incorporate wide areas of their interpersonal lives into usable, assimilated experience. Mental health professionals in child guidance clinics can observe these security operations in the process of formation, and also have opportunities of treating them before they become entrenched.

Mental health professionals accustomed to thinking in Freudian terms should note that the security operation of selective inattention differs significantly from the Freudian principle of repression. In repression something occurs in a person's life; he usually, but not always, is aware of it. However, owing to its painful nature it is forced out of his awareness and lodged in a division of the mind termed the unconscious mind. The repressed feeling, thought or experience may later come forth in a different form such as a psychiatric symptom or disturbed behavior; various mental mechanisms accomplish this transformation. Selective inattention, in contrast, *is always an ongoing process. A person can selectively inattend a thing only at the moment it is occurring; he cannot selectively inattend something that occurred in the past.* A selectively inattended incident cannot be stored away in a person's fund of experience since he was not aware of it when it happened; as indicated above, it is as if the incident never occurred. Hence, it cannot later erupt in the form of a symptom or disturbed behavior.

THE ORIGINS OF THE SELF-SYSTEM IN CHILDHOOD

Sullivan uses the term *self-system* to designate *all the security operations a person customarily employs to protect himself against anxiety; it thus embraces all the interpersonal activities of an individual for keeping his relationships with people comfortable.*

During the two decades during which he slowly developed his concept of the self-system, Sullivan used the expressions *self, self-dynamism* and *self-system* to designate it. He settled on the term *self-system* in the last years of his life. In its final form the self-system is quite different from his earlier concepts; failure to understand this can confuse readers of Sullivan's works.

The *self-system,* in a crude simile, may be likened to a circle of ramparts which defend an individual against assaults of anxiety; *security operations* are the components of which the ramparts are composed. This illustration errs, however, by suggesting that the self-system is rigid and fixed; it is in fact a continually flexible set of defenses against emotional pain.

Formation of the self-system begins in childhood; by the end of childhood some aspects of it may be well developed. Its evolution continues throughout the juvenile period and adolescence. In subsequent life it is modifiable, but its basic features tend to be fairly persistent after early adulthood. *The self-system grows as one security operation after another is developed throughout a person's formative years.*

When we deal with a person, we are continually in contact with his self-system. He constantly is using various security operations, from the total repertory of his self-system, to avoid emotional distress (anxiety) in his relationships with us. The self-system of an individual to a large extent identifies him as the person whom we know.

The nature of an evolving self-system becomes clear in the following example of a three-year-old child. Choosing an arbitrary number for ease in illustration, six of this child's security operations are 1) a tendency to lapse into stubborn silence when he encounters an emotionally threatening interpersonal situation, 2) obdurate resistance to the demands of older children and adults when there is tension between them and him, 3) withdrawal into solitary play when a stressful interpersonal state arises, 4) physical clinging to a familiar adult when he enters a new interpersonal situation, 5) flight into meticulous play with inanimate objects such as toys and coloring books when anxiety begins to occur in his relationships with children or adults, and 6) return to more immature levels of behavior, such as in speech and physical actions, when his emotional needs are not met by the people around him.

These six security operations, comprising a significant segment of his self-system, give us a fair picture of the kind of person this three-year-old child is at this point in his development. Anyone who has close contact with the child must deal with these security operations at various times, and if the relationship with the child is fraught with anxiety, that person encounters them almost continuously. This child has many other security operations which contribute to his self-system; if all of these security operations were to be described, we would have a still more extensive representation of this child.

Many other things besides his self-system and its component security operations form his personality structure and determine his interpersonal functioning. His capacities for giving and receiving affection, his abilities to conform to the ordinary demands of social living (toilet training, not breaking things, etc.), his level of intelligence as manifested in his dealings with people, particular skills and talents which integrate him with others, and many other features go into making him the sort of person he is.

However, these things dovetail closely with the constituents of his self-system. For example, his abilities to utilize his intelligence and special skills may be hampered or facilitated by how his security operations are intertwined with them. A child who under stress withdraws from people may not be able to employ his abilities. A child who in tense circumstances tries to ingratiate himself with people may utilize his intelligence and talents with special diligence to gain their approval.

A child's self-system is built up slowly in his interactions with the close people around him. Thus, the six security operations of the self-system of the child described above probably are being evolved in his attempts to deal with the emotional pain he experiences in his relationships with indifferent, hostile or harshly domineering parents. Whether this segment of his self-system becomes ingrained and is carried into adult life, or is considerably changed during later childhood, the juvenile period and adolescence, will be determined by the nature of his relationships with many persons in his home and outside it.

Sullivan emphasizes that the term self-system does not designate anything that actually exists in a person. It is merely a literary device employed to embrace the sum of a person's security operations. The expression security operation, in contrast, designates an actual interpersonal event which can be directly observed. For reasons similar to those dealt with in preceding parts of this chapter and in prior ones, the term self-system therefore is not in any sense similar to the Freudian term ego or kindred terms in other psychiatric systems.

Much of the work of psychiatrists and other mental health professionals deals with the ways in which security operations (and, in their totality, self-systems) of people operate in families, social groups and other interpersonal situations. Detecting and resolving problems of sick self-systems constitutes a major part of psychiatric treatment.

PARATAXIC EXPERIENCE IN CHILDHOOD

Sullivan adopted the term *parataxic distortion* from the work of the American psychologist and psychiatrist Thomas V. Moore; both were professionally active in the Washington-Baltimore area between 1922 and 1924. Over the next 20 years, Sullivan extensively altered his concept of parataxic distortions. We shall here consider parataxic experience in the way Sullivan discussed it in the final period of his life.

A parataxic experience occurs when a person treats another individual as if he were someone else from another segment of his life. The nature of a parataxic experience is made clear in the following simple example. A four-year-old child dominates his mother by temper tantrumish behavior and sullen withdrawal. This mobilizes much anxiety in his mother and she conforms to his demands in almost all situations. When he enters nursery school at the age of four, this child maintains the same interpersonal pattern in his relationship with the nursery school supervisor. As a result, conflicts arise between him and the supervisor, and his interpersonal adjustment with both the supervisor and other children in the school is impaired. This occurs because *he is dealing with the nursery school supervisor as if she were his mother. He is interacting with this new person as if she were someone from another segment of his life; he is behaving in a parataxic manner.*

In this particular situation the parataxic behavior at the nursery school and the relationship with the mother, which causes the parataxic distortion, are going on at the same time in the child's life. In most cases, the parataxic distortions which bring people to the attention of mental health professional workers are caused by relationships from the individual's *past*. For example, if subsequent experience does not modify this child's personality, in adulthood he will tend to manipulate his marital partner, social acquaintances and work associates by brow-beating and sullenness. His parataxic distortions will then assume the form in which they are most commonly encountered in psychiatric work.

The origins of most parataxic distortions lie in infancy, childhood and the juvenile period. If these parataxic difficulties are minor and cause little trouble in the person's interpersonal relationships, they may be considered within the broad range of normal limits. If they cause significant problems in his marital, familial, vocational and social life, he may be considered emotionally disturbed.

Unsound patterns of feeling, thinking and acting which arise in childhood and are capable of generating later parataxic difficulties may in many cases be corrected by subsequent, healthier interactions with people. If the temper-trantrumish behavior and sullen withdrawal of the child described above do not enable him to manipulate his father, siblings, teachers, play companions and others, and if his mother can see the unhealthiness of her relationship with him and modify it, he may lose this sick method of dealing with people and substitute sounder ways of relating to others. If the problem is so severe that his parents seek help in a child guidance clinic when he is five years old, or if he himself seeks psychotherapy when he is 25, this parataxic disorder may be ameliorated in a *professional* interpersonal relationship.

Sullivan, in his graphic way, says that in parataxic disorders "ghosts" from the past intrude in ongoing interpersonal relationships. The para-taxically upset person is not truly dealing with the individual in front of him, but with an "imaginary person" who has arisen out of his previous life.

Parataxic distortions are not limited to two-person situations. The child cited above behaves parataxically with the nursery school super-visor and the other children in the room as he attempts to control his environment. Moreover, parataxic behavior is rarely as simple as in the case illustrated here. Several kinds of parataxic feelings and acting may, in varying degrees of intensity, be occurring at the same time in an interpersonal relationship. Into each interpersonal situation a person carries all his prior experience, healthy and unhealthy.

People who do not understand fully Sullivan's conception of parataxic experience sometimes confuse it with Freud's conception of transference. The differences between these two concepts are dealt with in detail in our book *The Treatment Techniques of Harry Stack Sullivan;* lengthy repetition of them here would constitute a digression. A few points, however, may be emphasized. Freud, in his concept of transference, proposes that an individual relives a traumatic relationship or incident that occurred during the first seven years of his life. In a therapeutic transference he becomes conscious of much painful material from his unconscious mind and rids himself of residual effects of the childhood trauma.

Sullivan, in contrast, feels that nobody ever relives anything. A person merely tends to carry old, unhealthy patterns of behavior into new situations. A person does not concoct new ways of interpersonal life on the spur of the moment; in each new interpersonal relationship he draws on the total body of his past experience. If an individual tends to brawl with his work superiors because he fought with his parents throughout his formative years, he is not reliving anything. He is simply drawing on personality-forming experiences he had, and is carrying them into new situations. If he never had sound, gratifying experiences with authoritative persons, he cannot draw on such experience in adjusting to the demands of his current situation. This applies both to relationships in general and to professional relationships in psychotherapy.

THE BEGINNINGS OF CONSENSUAL VALIDATION

Sullivan utilizes the term *consensual validation* to designate the process by which a child acquires the feelings, thoughts and attitudes which are generally accepted in the group in which he lives. Though consensual validation may begin in late infancy, it becomes paramount in childhood, the juvenile period and early adolescence.

In consensual validation the child reaches a *consensus* with the people around him about some aspect of his life, and this consensus is *validated* in numerous interpersonal experiences with diverse persons. Consensual validation is illustrated in the following elementary example. A two-year-old child gradually arrives at a consensus with the people in his family, and with others, that the four-legged, furry animal about the house is called a "dog." This consensus is validated by many interpersonal incidents involving various people and numerous dogs. This is a cognitive example, involving a function often labeled intellectual. Of much more importance in personality development are those areas of consensual validation involving experiences which have strong emotional significance.

Consensual validations dealing with deep-seated feelings, thoughts and attitudes have much greater impacts on the interpersonal life of the developing child. They deal with all features of his personality and such things as "right" and "wrong," acceptable and unacceptable activities, and healthy and unhealthy ways of interacting with people. They embrace virtually the entire range of ideas and feelings a person has about himself, his life and the people and things that make up his world.

The term *consensual validation* is a stumbling block to many readers of Sullivan's works. In recent times the word consensus has acquired the meaning of a reasoned agreement reached by a group of people; this is not what Sullivan means by consensus. He employs this word to designate the slow acquisition of a complex feeling or concept through close interaction with persons in an individual's environment; the person usually is not articulately aware that he is achieving this consensus, or becomes aware of it only in retrospect many years later.

For example, in childhood and the years beyond, a person may acquire a consensus that members of a family should have close, affectionate feelings toward each other, or that it is wrong to exploit others, or that he himself is a worthwhile, useful individual. Such a consensus is gradually reached over a period of years in innumerable interactions with the close people about him and with others in broad interpersonal settings. He may, or may not, ever formulate this consensus clearly to himself or to anyone else.

The word *validation* is also misleading to many mental health professionals when they first encounter it in Sullivan's writings. It does not indicate proof of something by observation or experiment. It designates the gradual confirmation of a feeling, idea or attitude in many interpersonal incidents and relationships. For example, an individual's feeling that he is a valued, loved person is validated in innumerable events in which he is treated as a valued, loved person. By degrees he senses that this concept of himself is *valid*. In many cases this validated feeling is never put into words either by the person or anyone else around him; it simply becomes an imbued attitude because of the ways in which he is treated by important persons in his life and by others with whom he associates.

Consensual validation can be healthy or unhealthy. A child who is treated as an inadequate, unlovable individual by his parents and siblings slowly develops the consensually validated feeling that he is inferior and unworthy of love and respect. If, as a result, he is unable to form sound relationships with persons in his neighborhood, at school and in other situations, he will lack the kinds of interpersonal contacts which might correct this feeling. He has carried out of his home environment the feeling that close interpersonal associations are painful, and his isolation in nonfamily interpersonal settings makes his consensually validated attitude about himself more ingrained.

However, Sullivan feels that a consensually validated feeling, concept or attitude never becomes rigidly fixed. Later experience can always modify it in small or large ways. Thus, the person who carries out of his childhood years the feeling that he is inadequate may slowly develop a healthier view of himself in subsequent interpersonal life. If in his relationships in later interpersonal situations he is treated as a worthwhile, able, loved individual, he may in time arrive at a sounder consensual validation about himself and his capacities to interact with others. If consensually validated feelings, thoughts and attitudes could not be changed, psychotherapy, as well as spontaneous emotional growth in nontherapeutic settings, would be impossible.

The amount of consensual validation that goes on in childhood is vast; it involves almost every aspect of the child's feelings, thinking and interpersonal activity. Virtually everything a person does all his life, from childhood onward, is the result of complex networks of consensually validated feelings and ideas.

Syntaxic Experience and Consensual Validation. Sullivan divides all experience into prototaxic, parataxic and syntaxic modes.

As discussed in the first chapter, prototaxic experience consists of the fragmented, timeless, spaceless mode of existence that an infant has in the early months of his life. It gradually wanes as the infant, and later the child, organizes his concepts of objects, people and himself. After that, protataxic experience occurs only in panic states, nightmares, some forms of psychiatric illness and a few other states.

Parataxic experience, as outlined in the preceding section of this chapter, occurs when a person treats another individual as if he were someone from a prior segment of his life. Parataxic experience usually is unhealthy, but it may be so mild that it causes the individual little trouble in his interpersonal life; severe parataxic distortions cause major difficulties.

In *syntaxic* experience a person utilizes well adjusted, realistic feelings, thoughts and actions. Syntaxic experience is based upon a firm grasp of the actual state of a person's relatedness to people and things in his environment; it involves a fairly accurate appraisal of himself as a person with reasonable worth and self-esteem. Syntaxic thinking is facilitated by the development of language during childhood. Language helps a person crystallize his feelings and thoughts in clear ways; it helps him organize his experience into patterns in which events, relationships with people and a great deal of knowledge about the expanding world around him are integrated. Implicit in syntaxic experience are, in crude or refined ways, conceptions of cause and effect and of predictability in sequences of events involving both things and people. Except when prototaxic and parataxic experience displace it in emotional and interpersonal difficulties, syntaxic experience is the usual mode in which each person experiences the things that go on in his daily life.

Syntaxic experience and consensual validation go hand in hand. Thus, in the last example given above, the person who emerges from infancy and early childhood with the feeling that he is inadequate, worthless and unlovable achieves in later childhood and the juvenile period a sounder view of himself through the operation of syntaxic experience. He is enabled by it to view things more accurately, to see that the sick ways he was treated at home do not correspond to his true personality qualities and interpersonal abilities, and to evolve a healthier, consensually validated conception of himself.

By their very nature, syntaxic feelings, thoughts and actions are healthy. They are not contaminated by the unorganized features of prototaxic experience or the distorted qualities of parataxic experience.

As will be discussed in later chapters, in some psychiatric illnesses syntaxic experience crumbles and other kinds of experience are unleashed. Thus, prototaxic phenomena play a role in a schizophrenic process as the patient retreats from an interpersonal world which he has found intolerably painful, and parataxic distortions become prominent in some persons with paranoid states, sociopathic personality disorders and other forms of emotional maladjustment.

Chapter 4

The Therapeutic Implications
of Sullivan's Concepts of
Infancy and Childhood

Throughout his psychiatric career, Sullivan spent most of his time working with patients. After entering psychiatry in early 1922, he never held a position that was primarily administrative, and all his research activities involved close work with patients. His ideas about personality growth and emotional functioning were derived from things he could observe in the people he was treating.

As a result, his concepts of personality development and psychotherapy are interlocked. Almost everything in his scheme of personality evolution has direct bearing on various aspects of psychotherapy. In this chapter we shall examine some of Sullivan's therapeutic techniques which have particular relevance to his concepts of personality development in infancy and childhood. This will deepen our understanding of Sullivan's views on personality growth.

THE INTERPERSONAL NATURE OF PSYCHOTHERAPY:
PARTICIPANT OBSERVATION

Sullivan feels that since personality is formed in the context of ongoing interpersonal relationships, psychotherapy should proceed in essentially the same manner. In psychotherapy, one person, designated

46

the patient or client, seeks help for problems from another person who has expertise in such work. Therapy consists of vibrant dialogues in which the therapist listens, asks questions and makes statements as he and the patient examine many facets of the patient's difficulties.

The therapist is an alert *observer* of the dialogue in which he is *participating*. Hence, Sullivan employs the term *participant observation* to define the therapist's role, and his kind of treatment is *interpersonal psychotherapy*. *Participant observer* and *interpersonal psychotherapy* are as specific for Sullivan as psychoanalyst and psychoanalysis are for Freud.

Since personality problems arise in sick face-to-face interpersonal relationships, treatment is conducted in healthy face-to-face interviews. Sullivan rejects the concept of an aloof, uninvolved therapist who makes occasional interpretations or who acts as a screen onto which the patient projects his problems. Therapy is an energetic give-and-take procedure designed to broaden the patient's awareness of his problems and to enable him to solve them in his everyday interpersonal life.

Just as the words and acts of parents affect the feelings and actions of children, the verbal and nonverbal behavior of the therapist affects what the patient says and does. For example, the things a patient says and how he feels in an interview are much influenced by whether the therapist says, "Perhaps we might consider any problems you have with members of your family," or "Say with as little hesitation as possible everything that comes to mind," or "Tell me how you feel about entering psychotherapy." Further, the facial expressions, voice tones, body postures and other nonverbal acts of the therapist often are more important than what he says in determining the course of an interview. At all times the therapist vigilantly *observes* these things in the interview in which he is *participating;* he observes the feelings and actions of *both* the patient and himself.

In the same way in which parents and other adults should be tuned to the *needs* of infants and children, a therapist should be alert to note what the patient is seeking in therapy and what his interpersonal needs are. He never assumes, on the basis of theories about personality structure, what is occurring in the patient and in his day-to-day relationships with people. By questions, comments and strategic periods of silence, the therapist helps the patient to explore his life, both present and past. When he is in doubt about what the patient means, he investigates by specific questions, and in doing this both he and the patient broaden their awareness about some aspect of the patient's life. The therapist takes nothing for granted; he does not let unclear phrases and sentences go by, camouflaging from both the patient and himself the full meaning of what the patient is saying.

Sullivan stresses to the therapist that *you don't know until you find out,* and neither does the patient. He feels that in much psychotherapy 90 percent of what the patient says remains obscure because it is not examined in a vigorous to-and-fro dialogue; as a result, clear, substantiated conclusions are rarely reached about anything. Just as parents and other adults should talk things out with children and come to lucid understandings, therapists and patients should arrive at new clarifications about the events and relationships of the patient's life.

The principles of participant observation and the interpersonal nature of psychotherapy are particularly relevant to the child guidance clinic method of treating the emotional problems of children and adolescents by the simultaneous interviewing of parents and their children by different therapists. Since the children's difficulties are being produced by the sick interpersonal relationships in which they are being reared, treatment ideally should include all the involved persons. Sullivan's influence on the evolution of child guidance clinic techniques in the 1920s and 1930s was marked; his impact was as much by his teaching sessions and by word-of-mouth diffusion of his ideas among mental health professional workers, as by his writing. An extension of child guidance methodology was the development of family therapy in the 1950s, in which direct observation of interactions of parents and children in joint sessions offered a further option in the spectrum of interpersonal therapies.

Sullivan sometimes speaks of the *interpersonal geography* of a developing child. He utilizes this term to emphasize a child's needs for continuous contacts with people in a healthy interpersonal environment. In employing this expression he was anticipating the term *interpersonal ecology* which is currently being used.

THE THERAPEUTIC MANAGEMENT OF
PARATAXIC DISTORTIONS

As discussed in the preceding chapter, a parataxic experience occurs when a person treats another individual as if he were someone else from another segment of his life. For example, in the simple case vignette given in Chapter 3, a child manipulates his parents by demanding, temper-tantrumish behavior, and he attempts to dominate persons at nursery school and in subsequent life situations *as if they were his parents*. As a result, he has considerable problems in interpersonal adjustments because of this parataxic distortion. Most of the parataxic warps that cause trouble in living begin in the close interpersonal relationships of infancy, childhood and the juvenile period.

Psychiatrists and other mental health professional workers spend much of their therapeutic time dealing with parataxic problems that began in patients' formative years. In patients with passive personality disorders, aggressive personality problems, antisocial personality disturbances and many other personality difficulties, the patient's parataxic distortions constitute the major reason for therapy. In addition, in most patients with neurotic symptomatology, psychosomatic disorders, psychoses and various other kinds of psychiatric difficulty, parataxic disturbances lie behind the clinical syndrome which the patient presents; for example, a patient with a phobic neurosis or anxiety states may have passive parataxic problems underlying his neurotic symptomatology.

Sullivan feels that therapy need not in all cases trace the origins of parataxic problems to the childhood relationships in which they began. If the parataxic warp (a phrase Sullivan often uses) is mild or moderate, it may be necessary to deal with it only on the level of the patient's day-to-day experiences. For example, a person with a mild or moderate passive personality disorder may make much progress by examining the emotional causes and consequences of his passiviity in large numbers of his current interpersonal relationships. Therapy may thus deal with the patient's passivity in his marital situation, his relationships with his children, his work adjustment and other life settings.

In other cases, however, successful therapy demands investigation of how the patient's parataxic difficulties originated in unhealthy interactions in childhood and were worsened in subsequent interpersonal situations. Such therapy tends to be necessary in patients with severe parataxic problems, but there is no precise correlation between the degree of a parataxic warp and the need for exploration of its childhood beginnings.

A therapist may deal with a parataxic distortion in two general ways: 1) He may examine how the parataxic problem influences the patient's ongoing interpersonal life and arose during his formative years, and 2) he may work on the ways in which the parataxic warp affects the only relationship which is available for direct scrutiny—the relationship the patient sets up with the therapist. A patient brings into this relationship his characteristic ways of relating to people, and this includes, of course, his parataxic difficulties. For example, a patient with an aggressive parataxic problem tends to manipulate and control the therapist, and a patient with a passive parataxic tendency is inclined to be ingratiating and dependent toward the therapist. The patient and the therapist can explore how the parataxic problem unfolds as the patient-therapist relationship evolves. Both these basic approaches to the therapy of parataxes are utilized in many cases.

When a therapist treats patients in group therapy, family therapy, transactional analysis and other special groups, the patient's parataxic distortions may find expression in his interactions with other members of the group or with the therapist himself. Depending on the ways in which the group operates, the therapist, or other patients or the person himself may explore how such parataxic warps are influencing the patient's feelings, thoughts and actions in the group and in his daily life.

The ways in which management of a parataxic distortion in interpersonal psychotherapy differs much from the analysis of a transference reaction in Freudian psychoanalysis are covered in detail in Chapter 3.

THE MANAGEMENT OF ANXIETY

As pointed out in Chapter 2, Sullivan uses the term anxiety to indicate all forms of emotional pain; it embraces apprehensiveness, tension, panic, shame, guilt and other forms of emotional distress. Anxiety occurs when something is going wrong, or has long gone wrong, in the individual's interpersonal relationships; moreover, once present, anxiety blocks a person's capacity to be aware of what is occurring in his associations with others. The anxiety-laden event thus does not become part of the general body of assimilated experience upon which he can draw in his subsequent interpersonal dealings. As far as the person is concerned, it is as if the anxiety-ridden experience had never occurred.

The same thing occurs in psychotherapy. As the patient approaches an anxiety-laden area of his life, he tends to deviate from the subject or to camouflage it in ways that prevent him from coming to grips with it. During his formative years he found that any approach to the anxiety-filled area was dangerous; it flooded him with a discomfort that ranged from mild tenseness to devastating panic. One of the constant technical problems in therapy, therefore, is to keep the patient's emotional distress, or anxiety, at a low enough level to permit reasonably comfortable investigation of all aspects of his life which are relevant to his psychiatric difficulties. Sullivan spends a great deal of time in his published material discussing ways for reducing anxiety and thus maintaining the flow of an interview in useful ways.

One of the main tasks of therapy is to help the patient incorporate into his aware, assimilated experience many things which the anxiety he had in childhood prevented him from perceiving. In a sense, the childhood errors in living are corrected by incorporation of the childhood experiences which anxiety blocked him from absorbing. For example, the person who in childhood could not perceive the hostility and depreciation toward him by a rejecting parent because it was too painful to become aware of these things, achieves this awareness in psychotherapy, and is thus freed from the harmful impacts they had on his personality development and interpersonal functioning.

Another of the main goals of therapy is to decrease the amount of emotional discomfort the individual feels each time he encounters an interpersonal situation which he found distressing in childhood and has since then avoided. For example, the individual who cannot form close associations with people because the close relationships of his childhood were anxiety-laden, develops in therapy the capacity to enter into more comfortable contacts with people. The individual who fears that any close relationship will in time lead to rejection and abandonment gradually becomes free of this dread and is able to enter comfortably into relationships with people.

In some psychiatric illnesses the patient flees the pain of ongoing interpersonal life and returns, at least in part, to the noninterpersonal phase of early infantile experience. We shall discuss this in later chapters when we deal with panic states and schizophrenic disorders. In these illnesses one of the therapist's major aims is to bridge the gap between the patient and the interpersonal world from which he has retreated; he seeks to help him become more at ease in a wide range of interactions with people.

SECURITY OPERATIONS AND THE SELF-SYSTEM
IN PSYCHOTHERAPY

Security operations, the interpersonal attitudes and activities a person formed in childhood to avoid anxiety, offer both problems and opportunities in psychotherapy.

For example, the individual who during his formative years evolved marked passivity as a way to avoid anxiety in his interpersonal dealings tends to be ingratiating and obliging to the therapist. He discusses things which he senses the therapist feels are related to his problems, and he avoids material which he feels is contrary to the therapist's viewpoints. A passive person often becomes skillful in picking up verbal and nonverbal clues about a therapist's reactions, even when the therapist sits out of his direct field of vision. The therapist's voice tones, body rustlings, scratchings of notes, facial expressions when the patient enters and departs and other things guide the passive person into areas and attitudes which often are more relevant to the therapist's theories than the patient's problems. In such situations, Sullivan says, much pseudotherapy can go on for long periods of time.

However, when correctly handled, security operations provide much material for constructive work in therapy. The therapist deals with security operations in two principal ways: 1) He helps the patient explore how unhealthy security operations enable him to avoid emotional pain in his ongoing interpersonal associations, and how these security operations developed in close relationships with people during his formative years. 2) The patient and the therapist may examine how security operations function in the relationship between the two of them.

For example, 1) the patient and the therapist may unravel how the aggressiveness of a person with an aggressive personality disorder creates difficulties in his marriage, vocational situation and other current settings. They also may investigate how aggressiveness evolved as one of the patient's main ways of avoiding anxiety during childhood in his relationships with parents, siblings and others. 2) The patient and the therapist may explore how the patient uses irritable attacks and sullen evasiveness in the interview situation to prevent the examination of painful subjects and to avoid true collaboration in the therapeutic work.

As outlined in Chapter 3, Sullivan employs the term *self-system* to embrace all a person's security operations; it is not a thing, but merely a literary device which enables us to talk comprehensively about all the security operations which characterize an individual as he seeks to avoid anxiety in his day-to-day interpersonal life. Throughout treatment a therapist is almost constantly dealing with some aspect of the patient's self-system. Some feature of the self-system (in other words, some particular security operation) is at almost all times blocking therapeutic access to anxiety-laden events and relationships. An important aspect of therapy is to modify one or more features of the patient's self-system which are distorting his interpersonal relationships and are causing emotional difficulties. For example, at a particular moment in therapy the therapist may be seeking to help the patient become aware of how the security operation of selective inattention, a prominent feature of this patient's self-system, is blocking awareness of how his obsessive-compulsive rigidity with people is causing difficulties in his marriage.

Sullivan feels the patient should not be deprived of a characteristic way of dealing with people, even a sick anxiety-ridden security operation, unless the therapist can see his way toward replacing it with a healthy interpersonal pattern. He gives much attention to specific techniques for doing this.

THE THERAPEUTIC ROLE OF CONSENSUAL VALIDATION

In the same sense that a child grows interpersonally by consensual validation, a patient grows in emotional health by the consensual validation he achieves in therapy.

The operation of consensual validation in therapy is illustrated in the following simple example. After examining diverse aspects of a passive person's relationships with people, the therapist suggests, as a subject for exploration, that one of the patient's problems is the feeling that any assertiveness will alienate people from him and will lead to isolation. The therapist and the patient, often in a series of interviews, proceed to discuss interpersonal events in the patient's relationships with his marital partner, his parents, his children, his work associates, his social acquaintances and others to determine if one of the roots of the patient's passive personality problem is a dread that self-assertiveness will cause abandonment of him by these people. In time a consensus is gradually reached, and it is validated by still further exploration of this aspect of the patient's feelings, thoughts and interpersonal reactions during assertive activities.

Such consensual validation is not a coldly reasoned process; it consists of the slow assimilation of new ways of feeling, thinking and associating with people through investigation of what is going on in the patient's current life, and what has happened in his past. The same area of the patient's living is approached from many points of view. In most cases, consensual validation is a historical process. It deals with how the patient's ways of interacting with others have been molded by what happened to him in the past. In addition, it often considers the patient's future. Where will his unhealthy modes of living with others lead him in subsequent years if they are not modified? What new vistas of healthy interpersonal life will be opened to him if he can change his ways of relating to others ?

The underlying principle in all interpersonal psychotherapy is that there are no essential differences between the ways in which people get sick and the ways in which they get well. If unhealthy consensual validations play large roles in producing psychiatric difficulties, healthy consensual validations are the main ways in which people achieve better levels of adjustment.

In this chapter we have merely sketched the ways in which Sullivan's methods of treatment and his views on personality in infancy and childhood are interwoven. The exact ways in which these treatment techniques are applied in day-to-day therapy are covered in lengthy discussions scattered throughout Sullivan's published works, and a concise synopsis is presented in our book *The Treatment Techniques of Harry Stack Sullivan.*

Chapter 5

The Juvenile Period

The juvenile period begins when a child develops a strong need for close interpersonal activity with nonfamily children of his own age group; it ends when sexual maturation starts to exercise a marked influence on his interpersonal relationships. As a rule, Sullivan employs only these interpersonal criteria to indicate the boundaries of the juvenile period; however, for the sake of clarity we shall define it as beginning at four or five years of age and ending between 10 and 12.

Sullivan often separates the final part of the juvenile period off into a separate phase of development which he terms preadolescence. He feels that this phase varies much in length from one person to another; it may last from a few months to a couple of years. In this book we shall treat preadolescence as a subdivision of the juvenile period, for reasons we shall outline later in this chapter.

CONSENSUAL VALIDATION IN THE JUVENILE PERIOD

During the juvenile period a person spends steadily larger amounts of time outside his home, and the interpersonal bonds he forms with both children and adults in his neighborhood, at school and in other settings exert significant influences on his personality development. Some psychiatric writers feel that the years of later childhood have little impact on personality formation, but Sullivan stresses their importance.

56

The interpersonal associations which a person has in the broader settings of the juvenile period offer valuable opportunities for correcting personality warps that arose in the narrower home circle in which he previously spent most of his time. Thus, the child who emerges from the first several years of life with the feeling that he is an inadequate, inept person with little capacity for forming sound relationships with people may in his associations of the juvenile period evolve a much healthier view of himself. In general, if the individual's personality difficulties are not severe, his healthy experiences at school, in the neighborhood, in social groups and in other situations may erase the marks left by sick familial interactions. Sullivan feels that for some people the juvenile period is the most important epoch in their personality growth.

In favorable circumstances a majority of the other children with whom an individual associates during his juvenile years come from reasonably healthy homes and have sound personality structures. Close living with them hence tends to cancel out the adverse effects of damaging interpersonal situations present in his own home. Even when the children and adults in the juvenile's new environments have personality difficulties, they usually are different from the ones the juvenile has; hence, they are healthy in the areas in which he is unhealthy, and interaction among them helps the juvenile with his particular problems. In most cases, at least in our culture, the odds are that a person finds in the wider environments of the juvenile period interpersonal associations which help rather than harm him; the specific unhealthy influences of his home setting tend to be corrected by the diversity of healthy relationships in the continually broader situations into which he moves as the years of the juvenile period pass.

As Sullivan succinctly puts it, given favorable circumstances, people whose problems are not too severe gradually "cure" one another. All security operations (that is, all aspects of the self-system) and all forms of anxiety (emotional distress) can be altered in healthier directions.

Moreover, in the latter part of the juvenile period each juvenile group, large or small, begins to form its own consensual validations about itself and its ways of looking at things. It starts to carve out new concepts about the ways in which people should live with each other; it evolves its own consensually validated ideas about values, customs, life styles and many other things, and these new consensual validations may differ from those of their parents. This process is much accelerated during adolescence as the person transfers more of his emotional investments from his family and its immediate surroundings to independent adolescent groups.

During the juvenile period, personality warps formed in infancy and childhood often are brought into high relief; difficulties that were not apparent, or which at least did not cause significant interpersonal trouble in earlier years, may begin to cause marked maladjustments. For example, a child who feels that all close relationships are dangerous and painful, and who as a result shuns associations with new people, may not have marked problems until he is forced to enter broader environments at school, in the neighborhood and in other situations. For Sullivan, the juvenile period and adolescence are not testings of prior personality development, but clarifications of them. Things that can be hidden in the narrow circle of home and family often cannot be camouflaged in the wider settings of later years.

In addition, Sullivan points out that the kinds of interpersonal settings into which the juvenile enters when he steps outside his home affect his opportunities for emotional growth. It makes much difference whether he enters an environment in which poverty, exploitation and viciousness are prevalent, or a suburban atmosphere which encourages sound, comfortable associations with people. In emphasizing this aspect of the juvenile period in the 1920s and 1930s, Sullivan was anticipating trends which became prominent in psychiatry several decades later. It is not certain whether Sullivan introduced the term *the sick society,* but in his lectures and writings in the 1920s and 1930s he was one of the earliest mental health professionals, and certainly the most distinguished, to focus attention on this aspect of personality development. Protest about social deprivation is, of course, centuries old, but Sullivan was the first to cite unfavorable social conditions *as a psychiatric problem and to evolve a system of personality development which made this clear.*

THE NONFAMILIAL EXPANSION OF INTERPERSONAL LIFE

Sullivan views the small groups of juveniles that form at school, in the neighborhood and in other situations as microcosms of the nonfamilial interpersonal groups in which the individual will spend much of his later life. In these nonfamilial groups a person begins to develop capacities for *collaboration, competition* and *compromise* (Sullivan employs these words virtually as technical terms) that he will need for sound adjustments in school settings, work situations, social groupings and other nonfamilial contexts. An individual does not merely carry into nonfamilial situations the interpersonal capacities which he developed at home. *He develops new interpersonal abilities in nonfamilial groups of the juvenile period and later epochs; he grows in them.*

The child who is interpersonally isolated, or is reared in disturbed childhood environments during the juvenile period may emerge from his formative years with persistent defects in his abilities to collaborate, compete and compromise.

In the lectures and seminars which form the major body of Sullivan's published works, he spends a fair amount of time discussing the importance of the nonfamilial *we*. In it a person must acquire the ability to adjust to extrafamilial authoritative figures, whether they be older than himself or of his own age group. He must evolve ways of forming consensual validations with superiors, peers and subordinates, and this requires interpersonal skills that in many cases are different from those he developed in his family. In these activities an individual must be able to maintain his self-esteem while not damaging the self-esteem of others. If one or many members of a group are impaired in these interpersonal skills, the group is to some extent sick, and the sick group in turn further damages its members.

In the first quarter of this century, when most of the current psychiatric schools of thought were evolved, families were large and cohesive; these psychiatric systems accordingly stress family interactions and pay little attention to interactions outside the family. Divorce, geographical mobility and work outside the home by both parents were uncommon then, and are prevalent now. A child today spends much more time outside the home and apart from his parents and siblings than he did in earlier decades. Sullivan's stress on the impacts of nonfamilial relationships on personality development has therefore acquired steadily mounting relevance.

Interpersonal Isolation and Ostracism. Sullivan views interpersonal isolation, or the threat of it, as a strong painful force which drives an individual to seek associations with people, even when such associations are anxiety-ridden. He uses the word loneliness, indicating the absence of interpersonal life, as a specialized term in discussing isolation. Loneliness is exceptionally damaging during the juvenile period, for this is the time when the child should be acquiring a broad spectrum of new interpersonal skills in his first push outward into nonfamilial areas of living. The absence of sound, vibrant relationships in nonfamilial circles at this time may leave a person persistently crippled; he may go into adolescence and adulthood without the necessary capacities for forming close associations with others; these deficiencies in turn separate him even more from people.

Interpersonal isolation, or loneliness, may be the product of various kinds of emotional damage. The person may emerge from his years of infancy and childhood with the feeling that close associations with people are dangerous and painful; participation in the fast-moving, exhilarating juvenile world disturbs him. In other cases the juvenile may feel that he is an inadequate, inept person who would fail if he tried to establish close contacts with people. Closeness with persons of the same sex, or the opposite sex, may be particularly threatening to some juveniles. In most cases, however, additional factors cause a person to go through his juvenile years in solitary, uninvolved ways, and prevent the ordinarily helpful features of this epoch from aiding him. The parental hostility, depreciation and rejection which contributed so much to his difficulties may continue to batter him throughout this period; if strong enough, it may hinder constructive experiences in the nonfamilial world of the child. A few children are for special reasons restricted to largely adult environments, or pass their juvenile years in remote areas in which their contacts with juvenile groups are limited or distorted.

Even more devastating is enforced isolation, which Sullivan terms *ostracism*. This occurs when a child who otherwise would move into juvenile circles is deliberately shunned because of socioeconomic, cultural or other reasons. Ostracism can produce long-lasting defects in a person's capacities of collaboration, competition, compromise and other interpersonal abilities which usually are acquired in juvenile groups.

THE EVOLUTION OF THE PERSONIFIED SELF

Sullivan uses the term *personified self* to indicate all the things a person can describe about himself. To a large extent it designates the same thing that is sometimes called the self-image, or the conscious self-image. An individual first begins to have articulate awareness of his personified self during the juvenile period, and it has marked effects on his subsequent personality development and interpersonal functioning.

Four areas are of particular importance in the personified self. 1) What does a person value about himself, and what does he disparage? 2) What sorts of things does he *deliberately* do to recover his self-esteem after something has made him feel anxious or inadequate? 3) To what extent is he aware of the kinds of experiences that make him feel uncomfortable and depreciated, and how does he deal with them to reestablish his emotional security? 4) How aware is he of his emotional reserves and the interpersonal resources on which he draws in times of stress? Under this last category Sullivan includes such things as the ways in which a person justifies his life and important actions, and any exalted purposes which he expresses in actions as well as thoughts and words.

A person's view of himself, whether it is realistically justified or not, strongly affects how he interacts with other people; his relationships with them are influenced by whether he sees himself as valued and able, or worthless and inept, or troublesome and guilt-laden. He carries into each interpersonal relationship a concept of what kind of person he is, and this has a marked effect on what he does in that relationship, and what its outcome is.

A person's personified self, or concept of himself, is molded to a large extent by the attitudes which the important people in his life have toward him during his formative years; their feelings toward him during the long stretch of the juvenile period are particularly significant. A child who is treated as worthwhile, loved and able tends to view himself as such, and a child who is treated as inferior, unlovable and inept is inclined to see himself in that light. Sullivan states that the personified self is mainly composed of "reflected appraisals." In these appraisals nonverbal attitudes and actions are usually as important as verbal ones.

A person may rectify unhealthy aspects of his personified self during the juvenile period. The child who in his home environment formed a concept of himself as inadequate and valueless may in the broader interpersonal circles of the juvenile period gradually see himself in a healthier way. A child who has emerged from his early years with the view that he is superior to others and entitled to dominate them may in the juvenile world develop a sounder perception of himself and his roles with others. Therapeutic experiences of this kind as a rule occur only when the distortions in the person's personified self are mild or moderate. If his personified self is grossly malformed he is prone to have marked difficulties with people outside his home. He is as a result unable to participate constructively in the juvenile interactions which might help him lose his distorted views of himself.

A person's personified self affects his attitudes toward others. An individual who sees himself in derogatory ways, derived from the hostility and rejection he experienced during his formative years, is inclined to see others in derogatory, hostile ways, though such feelings often are hidden behind a façade of apparently different attitudes. As a rule, only a person with secure self-esteem can have sound affection and respect for others, for how an individual views himself influences how he feels about human beings in general. This gives an individual's personified self an added dimension of importance in his interpersonal life.

The personified self should be clearly distinguished from such concepts as the emotionally comfortable (good) me, the anxiety-ridden (bad) me and the panic-ridden (not) me which are discussed in the last section of Chapter 1. The personified self embraces only those things which a person *can articulately describe about himself,* no matter how crudely he does it. The emotionally comfortable (good) me, the anxiety-ridden (bad) me and the panic-ridden (not) me are much more profound aspects of a personality structure, and an individual usually is unable to become aware of many aspects of them; the panic-ridden (not) me is entirely beyond articulate expression. Other differences are covered in Chapter 1.

AWARENESS AND UNAWARENESS IN THE JUVENILE YEARS

One of the effects of the greatly expanded interpersonal world of the juvenile period is that the individual, in his concentration on the diverse ongoing and recently past events of his life, loses acute awareness for things that happened in his past. The incidents and relationships of infancy and early childhood recede from his field of awareness and easy recall. In colloquial terms, they are "forgotten." Anxiety abets this process; experiences which are painful to recall become increasingly inaccessible to the individual.

Selective inattention, the security operation discussed in Chapter 3, becomes more active as a person passes through his juvenile years. His experience becomes more scattered, varied and diverse, and he is selectively unaware of increasingly large segments of it. More interpersonal events are happening per unit of time with a constantly larger number of people. Other security operations exclude from awareness things which are emotionally uncomfortable. As a result, there is a progressive constriction of the person's capacity to bring into clear awareness a large spectrum of things which have occurred in his past and are going on in his present life.

At this point it is necessary to deal with Sullivan's concepts of *awareness* and *unawareness.* Since he does not accept the concept of *mind* in psychology and psychiatry, he does not, of course, employ such ideas as the conscious mind and the unconscious mind. Instead, he utilizes the concepts of awareness and unawareness. This distinction is crucial; it should not be dismissed as trifling with words.

The nature of awareness and unawareness is best explained in a simple example.

A student in clinical psychology who is typing out a case report for presentation at a group conference the following day is operating at various levels of awareness. As his fingers skip along the keys of the typewriter he does not think out each movement. He is *unaware* of the intricate motions of his fingers. When, some years previously, he was learning to type, he carefully thought out each movement; at that time he *was aware* of the actions of each finger as it hit the keys. He is at this moment only aware that he is formulating the data for the case presentation.

On deeper levels he is *unaware* of many other things. He may, for example, be unaware of his apprehensiveness that he may not present his material well and, thus, be criticized by his colleagues and superiors. In addition, he may at the moment be unaware that his urgent feelings that he must do a good job are influenced by competition between him and one of his colleagues for a job offer that will be made in a few months' time. *These things are not in his ongoing field of awareness, but they could be brought within his awareness by personal reflection or by the comments of an observant friend.*

Other things may be so painful that they could be brought into his field of awareness only with some difficulty. He may have been reared by a critical father and a rejecting mother who bred in him a desperate need to prove by continual achievement his worthwhileness and ability; he feels constantly driven to demonstrate this both to himself and others. These feelings, the products of much past experience, goad him as he types his report. This facet of his personality may be so painful that he could become aware of it only with much difficulty.

The degrees of awareness in the feelings, thoughts and attitudes of a person are much more complex than those sketched here. However, this example illustrates the nature of Sullivan's concepts of *awareness* and *unawareness*. *Awareness* and *unawareness are merely characteristics of any feeling, thought or attitude.* Just as a feeling, thought or attitude may be important or trivial, strong or weak, it may be *aware* or *unaware*.

Anxiety (emotional pain) determines how accessible a feeling, thought or attitude is to a person. If the feeling or memory is fairly comfortable, a person can without much difficulty bring it into his field of awareness. If it is distressing, or perhaps panic-ridden, he may be able to draw it into his focus of awareness only with much difficulty, or not at all. He may be able to become aware of it only with the aid of a professional therapist. If the feeling, thought or memory provokes profound distress for him, the task of the therapist may require much skill, and in some cases awareness of highly disturbing material may be unwise.

It is during a person's juvenile period that awareness and unawareness begin to draw major attention from psychiatrists, clinical psychologists and other mental health professionals. From this point onward, awareness and unawareness are major considerations in evaluation of all the aspects of the personality structure and emotional problems of a person. They have been operative, of course, during late infancy and throughout childhood, but the inarticulateness and limited abilities of infants and young children make their roles less conspicuous, and perhaps less important. From the juvenile period onward, a person's capacity to be aware of important facets of his emotional and interpersonal life is an important factor in his psychological health or sickness. This subject will receive more attention in Chapter 7 when we consider the therapeutic implications of Sullivan's concepts of the juvenile period and adolescence.

THE PRINCIPLE OF RECIPROCAL EMOTIONS

In his *principle of reciprocal emotions,* Sullivan organizes many aspects of interpersonal life which we have so far dealt with separately. He draws them together in this principle and thus provides a useful tool for comprehensive examination of the complexities of interpersonal life. This principle applies to all close, prolonged relationships from earliest infancy onward, but in the juvenile period we can for the first time see it operating in the manner in which it will function for the rest of the person's life.

We shall discuss this principle in two-person situations, for it can be most clearly presented in this way. However, it operates in all close relationships, even though several or more people may be involved.

The principle of reciprocal emotions states that in every inter-personal relationship:

1) the *needs* of each person are met or not met,
2) the *interpersonal patterns* of the involved persons develop in healthy or unhealthy ways, and
3) each person forms *expectations of satisfaction or nonsatisfaction of his future needs.*

Needs. Each person has two basic kinds of needs—physical and interpersonal. An individual's physical needs, from the interpersonal point of view, are most pressing in infancy, since he must be fed, cleaned and in other ways cared for at a time when he cannot do these things for himself and must depend on close associations with others. By the time he reaches the juvenile period, he can do these things for himself, but their satisfaction, at least in our culture, rarely presents urgent difficulties.

Once the physical necessities of infancy and early childhood recede into the past, the most important needs of a person, in terms of personality development, are interpersonal. Each individual requires firm, affectionate relationships which are relatively free of emotional distress (anxiety). Many kinds of sound interactions with people are necessary to give him emotional security and the means for dealing with whatever kinds of anxiety he experiences. He needs continual opportunities for healthy consensual validation on a wide spectrum of major and minor things. Without such opportunities he risks the gradual warping of his personality and his ways of relating to people. An active, constructive life with people is important in preserving his self-esteem, for protecting him against isolation and for giving meaning to his life.

Interpersonal Patterns. Out of the innumerable events in which needs are satisfied, interpersonal patterns gradually develop. The person who finds affection and esteem in his relationships with important people gradually acquires a pattern of warm, comfortable closeness with others. The child, and later the juvenile, who in large numbers of incidents is depreciated, criticized and rejected, in time evolves a pattern of withdrawal from people, or chaotic rebellion against them, or some other unhealthy reaction.

The principle of reciprocal emotions continues to function in all important associations throughout life. It operates in marital relationships, vocational settings, social interactions and other situations. In every case, each person has *needs* to be met, and depending on their satisfaction or nonsatisfaction, *interpersonal patterns* and *expectations* of the future will be formed. These later operations of the principle of reciprocal emotions are much influenced by the basic patterns the involved persons have brought out of their formative years, but each new situation has its special features and particular ways in which *needs, patterns* and *expectations* are affected.

Expectations of Satisfaction or Nonsatisfaction of Future Needs. Sullivan, unlike some psychiatric pioneers, gives much attention to the *future*. He points out that many things a person does each day are determined by what he feels *will happen* as results of his feelings, thoughts and actions. The traumatized child does not go to his parents when he has trouble, for he feels he will receive only criticism and depreciation, whereas the healthily reared child seeks their aid because he expects help.

Casting a brief glance forward to adolescence and adulthood, a person's expectations of future events greatly affect whether he strives for achievements or retires from competition with his peers, seeks relationships with persons of the opposite sex or shuns them, and engages in or desists from a wide range of interpersonal activities.

Up to this point, the principle of reciprocal emotions merely draws together into one concept many things we have previously considered separately. The most important aspect of this principle is indicated by the word *reciprocal*. Each interpersonal relationship is much more complex than the simple examples given above. In each relationship there is a continuous to-and-fro flow of feelings, attitudes and actions.

From moment to moment, what one person does influences what the other does in return; the responses of each person affect what happens in the other one. Actions and reactions go back and forth vigorously. People mold each other's behavior. Every interpersonal incident, no matter how brief or trivial, has a history, and that history consists of the reciprocal actions and reactions of the involved people.

Both (or all) people involved in any interpersonal event have their needs, patterns and expectations. We have tended so far to look at interactions from the viewpoint of the child, but his parents, or the other persons with whom he is associating, also have their needs, evolving patterns and expectations. What the infant, or child, or juvenile feels, thinks and does has a marked effect on what happens next in the adult.

Herein lies one of Sullivan's prime achievements. He is interested in individuals, but he is equally interested in what goes on between them in the vibrant exchanges which continually modify the feelings, attitudes and acts of the participating persons. Just as Adam Smith "discovered" the market, and by examining what went on in its constantly fluid activity founded the science of economics, Sullivan "discovered" *the interpersonal field,* and by studying its never-ceasing, to-and-fro movements founded the science of interpersonal psychology and psychiatry.

The operation of *the principle of reciprocal emotions* in *the interpersonal field* may be illustrated in the two relatively simple illustrations which follow. The first illustration concerns a mother and her infant child, and the second involves a father and his juvenile son.

A mother who is entangled in a tense situation with her own critical, domineering mother *needs* affectionate responses, or relaxed satisfaction, from her infant after nursing and during other activities with the child. If, because of her apprehensiveness, she upsets the infant and does not get these *reciprocal* reactions from him, she may become anxious, or depressed, or irritable, or rejecting in her contacts with the child. The *interpersonal pattern* she sets up with the child may be unhealthy for both of them. It, moreover, affects her expectations of *future* satisfactions or nonsatisfactions from the child. Thus, as the child's *needs, patterns* and *future expectations* are being formed, the mother's are similarly being molded as feelings, thoughts and actions crisscross between them. These patterns in each of them may, unless healthier things occur between them, be carried into later years as the child passes through childhood, the juvenile period and later epochs.

In the second case, a father *needs* special responsiveness from his eight-year-old son as the father goes through a traumatic divorce. Simultaneously, the son *needs* particular affection and support from his father as he enters a new school situation after the divorce, and he also *needs* extra help in adjusting to the collapse of his parents' marriage. Each one, embroiled in his own difficulties, fails to meet the other's needs, and a *pattern* of anxious withdrawal occurs in both the father and the son. Also, the *expectations* of what he can get from close people in times of emotional stress in the *future* are adversely affected. The disappointed father becomes critical of his son for reasons of which he is not clearly aware, and the son feels hostility and rebelliousness toward this adult who has failed him; he may carry this problem into relationships with nonfamily adults at school and into other situations.

In each of these simple case vignettes, no one is *aware* of what is going on in *the interpersonal field* in which he is involved, as the *process of reciprocal emotions* sweeps him along. Just as the unawareness of each person is contributing to his emotional damage, the development of better awareness could help the ongoing interchange to alter in healthier ways.

Each of these situations is, of course, much more intricate than outlined here. In the first case the mother's relationship with her husband may be helpful or harmful in yet another current of crisscrossing feelings and attitudes in the general interpersonal field, and still other persons are probably involved. In the second case, both the constructive or destructive influence of teachers and children in the new school and the supportive or nonsupportive roles of the father's parents during the readjustment after his divorce may have far-reaching impacts in the broader reaches of the interpersonal field.

The study of these interpersonal fields, with the aim of helping all the involved people, constitutes much of the work of psychiatrists and other mental health professionals.

PREADOLESCENCE AND THE PERSON'S FIRST
CLOSE NONFAMILY RELATIONSHIPS

Sullivan inserted between the juvenile period and adolescence an epoch of personality development which he called *preadolescence*. Many writers on Sullivan find the concept of preadolescence controversial; others, including ourselves, consider it invalid.

We shall consider preadolescence from three viewpoints: 1) Sullivan's concepts of preadolescence, 2) objections to Sullivan's views on preadolescence and 3) a revised conception of preadolescence which seems to us more in keeping with what actually occurs in the terminal phase of the juvenile period.

Sullivan's Concept of Preadolescence. Sullivan felt that preadolescence began at quite diverse ages in different persons. It could begin as early as eight and a half years of age or as late as 11 or 12, and it could last from a few months to two or three years. It ended when physical sexual maturation began and genital sexual feelings started to be prominent.

The main characteristic of preadolescence, and the thing that marked its beginning, was a strong need for a close relationship with a nonfamily person of the same sex. There was a certain exclusiveness in this relationship; while it lasted it was the most important relationship in the late juvenile's life. Sullivan employed the now somewhat obsolete term *chum* for this close nonfamily person, and he used the expression *chumship* to designate the relationship.

In the preadolescent chumship a person experienced a set of feelings which Sullivan termed *intimacy*. He defined intimacy as a state in which an individual felt that the well-being of another person was as important to him as his own welfare. The two involved persons, or preadolescent chums, spent much time together, revealed their feelings and thoughts to each other much more fully than they had in any previous relationship, and had an interest in the well-being of the other individual that was stronger than that which they had had for the well-being of any prior person.

A healthy chumship was nonsexual in the genital sense of the word. Any genital sexual feelings or acts between the chums were unhealthy contaminants of their relationship. In the vast majority of chumships sexual genital urges did not occur.

Sullivan felt that, because of the closeness of the chums, their extensive discussions of their life experiences and feelings, and their dedication to each other's welfare, a chumship offered broad opportunities for correction of parataxic distortions formed in previous living. It also facilitated sound consensual validation on many features of each one's life, past and present. A good chumship, therefore, tended to be therapeutic for each member.

The chums spontaneously drifted apart when physical sexual maturation began; each of them tended to shift his main emotional investments to persons of the opposite sex during early and middle adolescence. They might remain friends, but their association lost its former intensity. Moreover, the interpersonal world of each one expanded rapidly and embraced relationships with many new persons of both sexes throughout early adolescence.

Sullivan felt that the special closeness of a chumship prepared a person for similar closeness with members of both sexes in the subsequent periods of adolescence and adulthood. Having once experienced an intense collaborative relationship with a nonfamily person of his own age, he was ready for similar relationships with other individuals in subsequent life epochs.

The importance of Sullivan's concept of intimacy, a feeling in which the well-being of another person is as important to an individual as his own welfare, takes on special meaning as the juvenile period (and its subdivision, preadolescence) ends and adolescence begins. The union during adolescence of the drive for intimacy with genital sexual drives produces an emotional and interpersonal force of great strength. It remains an important force for most of the rest of the individual's life.

Sullivan felt, moreover, that lack of a sound chumship in the late juvenile period (that is, in preadolescence) left a person poorly equipped for forming close relationships with persons of both sexes in later life stages. Since he did not develop the capacity for comfortable, collaborative intimacy in preadolescence, the best period for acquiring this ability, he was prone to have trouble in evolving this intimacy during adolescence and adulthood.

Objectitions to Sullivan's Views on Preadolescence. There are various objections to Sullivan's concept of preadolescence.

Firstly, when the developments of large numbers of children are surveyed, there is little evidence to support his concept. In child guidance clinic work with persons in the age bracket of eight-and-a-half to 11 or 12, such intense, exclusive relationships are not found in the majority of cases. The girl or boy who is passing through these years may have close associations with other persons of his own age, but the concentrated, quite special type of association that Sullivan outlined is infrequently encountered. Moreover, psychotherapy with adolescents and adults, in which earlier stages of the patient's life are examined, will rarely reveal a clear-cut preadolescent period of the kind Sullivan proposed.

Secondly, Sullivan's concept of preadolescence raises the uncomfortable question of the extent to which distinguished psychiatric innovators allow their own life histories to influence their views on personality development. For example, was Jung's formulation of a system of psychology and psychiatry which allows incorporation of religious views, and even encourages them to some extent, influenced by the fact that his father and nine of his uncles were clergymen? Did Freud's closeness to his mother and less intense relationship with his father play roles in molding his concept of the Oedipus complex? Similar questions can be asked about the systems of other eminent pioneers in psychology and psychiatry.

As outlined in the first chapter of our book *Harry Stack Sullivan: His Life and His Work,* Sullivan was an only child and had a lonely childhood and early juvenile period in a rural area. Then, during a two- or three-year period, he passed through a phase similar to that which he later was to describe as preadolescence. Strangely, both the isolated farm boys involved in Sullivan's preadolescent chumship became psychiatrists in their adult years.

Thirdly, in the final year or two of his life Sullivan seemed to be putting less emphasis on preadolescence. Even more important, he appeared to be pushing the beginning of intimacy forward a few years into early adolescence. This would make his system of personality development consistent with more widely held views on personality evolution in which intense, self-giving feelings (intimacy) tend to go hand in hand with the development of genital sexual feelings.

Rejection of Sullivan's concept of preadolescence does not, in our opinion, detract from the validity of the main lines of his scheme of personality development. There are precedents for this. Few Freudians accept Freud's concept of the death instinct, and there are publications of Jung which even his most devoted adherents consider invalid. Other examples could be given. It is unusual for a pioneer thinker to evolve a comprehensive system which does not, in time, require revisions and the rejection of some parts of it. Blanket acceptance of the ideas of a distinguished thinker smacks more of cultism than science.

A Revised Conception of Preadolescence. In our opinion, Sullivan's views on the late juvenile period (preadolescence) become valid if they are broadened and restated as follows. *In the final phase of the juvenile period, immediately preceding the beginning of adolescence, an individual's relationships with nonfamily persons of his own age bracket often acquire new intensity and become equal to family associations, or even more important than them, in their emotional impacts. This prepares the person for movement into adolescence, in which nonfamily relationships become paramount.* Intimacy, in which another person is as important to an individual as himself, may begin to evolve in the late juvenile period, but its full maturation occurs in adolescence and adulthood.

Casting a glance forward to adolescence, the union of the drives for intimacy and genital sexuality in a relationship with a person of the opposite sex, is a major feature of late adolescence and adulthood. A person's ability to achieve and sustain this combination of drives is one of the features by which we measure his emotional and interpersonal maturity.

Chapter 6

Early and Late Adolescence

Adolescence begins when physical sexual maturation begins to affect a person's relationships with people; it ends when he or she takes on the wide range of social, vocational and economic commitments which characterize adulthood. In approximate age numbers, in our culture adolescence starts between 11 and 13 and terminates in the early twenties.

Sullivan divides this period into *early* and late *adolescence.*

Early adolescence extends from the commencement of physical sexual maturation to the time when the individual establishes a stable pattern for expressing his genital sexual feelings. This stable pattern does not require regular sexual activity in the physical, genital sense; it merely demands a firm orientation in the manner and direction in which sexual urges will have their manifestations. Early adolescence thus ends at about 15 or 16.

Late adolescence begins with the achievement of a stable interpersonal sexual pattern and ends when a person assumes the activities characteristic of adulthood.

PERSONALITY GROWTH IN ADOLESCENCE

Adolescence is a period of continuing personality growth; it is not simply an era in which the soundness of previous personality evolution is tested, or a turbulent transition phase in which no true emo-

74

tional development occurs. Sullivan emphasizes, of course, the stresses of adolescence, but he gives much attention to the possibilities for emotional and interpersonal expansion in it.

Biological changes push this interpersonal development. A significant aspect of these biological changes is a marked increase in the capacity for sensuous feelings in the areas where skin and mucous membranes join. These include the genitals and the secondary sexual regions such as the mouth and other areas. These capacities for sexual arousal act as strong drives toward the diverse kinds of emotional and interpersonal activity which fall under the broad umbrella of sexual behavior. Although he recognizes that some arousal of the genitals, and perhaps the secondary sexual areas, can occur at times during infancy, childhood and the juvenile period, Sullivan feels that sexual urges play a negligible role in emotional and interpersonal life until the beginning of adolescence. In this he obviously differs much from the viewpoints held by Freudian and neo-Freudian schools.

Throughout adolescence a person's circles of interpersonal life become wider and more diverse. His opportunities for consensual validation and the resolution of parataxic distortions are enhanced by his participation in new, various kinds of interpersonal relationships with increasing numbers of people. This is one aspect of the possibilities for personality growth in adolescence. This is, of course, a continuation of the same process that began in the juvenile period; further specific opportunities for this process to operate will be discussed as we proceed to consider all that occurs during the adolescent years.

As pointed out also in our coverage of the juvenile period in the preceding chapter, an individual's personality growth in new non-familial settings is influenced by the healthiness or sickness of the environments he finds about him; parataxic warps are unlikely to be corrected in deprived, vice-ridden slums, and sound consensual validations are improbable in turbulent, unstable atmospheres.

Sullivan is the only distinguished psychiatric pioneer who gives some attention to *chance* in personality development. If personality is defined as the sum of an individual's interpersonal relationships and their emotional and ideational concomitants, the particular cultural and socioeconomic world into which life thrusts him has great influence on the kind of person he becomes. The ways in which blind chance helps or buffets a person affect his interpersonal living.

This point should not be dismissed as a mere statement of the obvious. Various psychiatric schools imply, if their doctrines are carefully scrutinized and thought out, that once personality is laid down during infancy and childhood the person's life is more or less mapped out, or at least restricted to certain well-defined possibilities. Sullivan rejects this as a marked oversimplification of what actually happens in life.

All these things become of increasing importance as the person progressively moves out of his parental home and its immediate setting into the broader community throughout adolescence.

A person's anxiety, in all its forms of emotional discomfort, affects his capacity to develop during adolescence. When anxiety is great and constricts the individual's interpersonal world, his growth during this period may be much hampered. When it is mild or moderate, he can, by alert participation in diverse interpersonal settings, mend many of the parataxic distortions he has brought out of traumatic experiences of infancy, childhood and the juvenile period. An individual often can come to grips with his emotional distresses and can see his problems in new ways as he broadens his insights into the ways in which people healthily interact with each other; he thus can evolve new ways of feeling, thinking and relating to others. This process can continue into early adulthood and even later periods in some persons.

We are here talking about the things that can occur spontaneously in personality development. Beyond this, of course, are the possibilities of therapeutic intervention by mental health professional workers, but that aspect of personality evolution lies outside our present field of attention.

SEXUALITY, LUST AND INTIMACY

In the psychiatric circles in which Sullivan worked in the Washington-Baltimore area and in New York, the word sexuality had a predominantly Freudian meaning. It concentrated on the diverse kinds of sensual experience in oral, anal, genital and other regions from birth through resolution of the Oedipus complex at the age of six or seven. As discussed above, that is not what Sullivan means by the term sexual.

To avoid confusion and to emphasize that he viewed sexuality in a quite different way, Sullivan employed the word *lust*. *Lust embraces all feelings, thoughts and interpersonal actions which have genital sexual activity as their immediate or distant goal. Lust becomes a major force in emotional and interpersonal life at the beginning of adolescence, or perhaps shortly before then.*

The phrase *genital sexual activity* in this definition includes activities in which the genitals of one or two persons are involved; it hence covers masturbation and any kind of genital contact between persons of opposite or the same sexes. The phrase *immediate or distant goal* covers genital urges whose physical expression may be possible only in the distant future, or perhaps never; it thus embraces all kinds of genitally oriented arousal from direct genital-to-genital intercourse to chaste courtship or passionate daydreaming in which genital-to-genital activity may be long delayed or perhaps may never occur. The term lust is both specific and broad.

Sullivan's concept of *intimacy* is discussed in the last section of the preceding chapter, but it must be considered again here since its main impact occurs during adolescence and beyond. As indicated there, *intimacy exists when a person feels that the well-being of another individual is as important to him as his own welfare.* Sullivan feels that the first intimate relationships in a person's life often occur during the final phase of the juvenile period, but that at this time they occur between persons of the same sex. By close, shared activities and much intense talk about what they are experiencing and have experienced, the persons in an intimate relationship grow emotionally.

Intimacy and lust are distinct, separate forces. Sullivan considers them to be two of the seven major *integrating forces* which draw the developing person and other people together in close interpersonal relationships during personality evolution. Some of these *integrating forces* persist throughout life. Lust is the last of these seven integrating forces to develop. In the succeeding section of this chapter we shall list these integrating forces and describe their operation from early infancy to adulthood.

In healthy personality development lust does not contaminate the close friendships of the late juvenile period. Any lustful contamination, producing a tendency toward long-lasting genital homosexuality in this period and beyond it, is, Sullivan states, "an error in development." He recognizes, of course, that transitory genital play among persons of the same sex is common in the juvenile period, but when true intimacy is joined to persistent lust in a late juvenile relationship an unhealthy development is occurring. The development of a persistent homosexual adjustment in adolescence and adulthood is more complex than this, of course, and will be considered in Chapter 13.

As briefly mentioned in the preceding chapter, *in adolescence intimacy and lust combine to produce a joint force which draws persons of the opposite sexes into strong relationships. This combination of intimacy and lust is one of the main characteristics of adolescence, and once achieved it remains one of the most powerful interpersonal stimuli for the rest of the individual's life.*

It is now clear why Sullivan divides adolescence into *early adolescence* and *late adolescence*. During early adolescence the individual is gradually linking lust and intimacy in a comfortable, healthy way; he or she achieves this in three or four years. *Late adolescence* begins when this is accomplished and the person has established a stable pattern for the expression of his genital sexual urges in relationships which are intimate or are capable of becoming intimate.

In relationships between persons of opposite sexes in which intimacy and lust are comfortably joined, the involved persons have extensive opportunities for consensual validation and the correction of parataxic distortions. Such consensual validation and correction of parataxes become stronger in adolescence and early adulthood than during previous epochs. The linked persons share experiences, past and present, and talk and work things out together in a manner neither has previously experienced so intensely. This is another one of the factors that enables adolescence to be an era of emotional growth. Verbal and nonverbal features are equally important in successful adolescent relationships combining intimacy and lust.

From late adolescence onward, an individual's emotional health depends to a large extent on how successfully he satisfies his needs for 1) intimacy, 2) lust, 3) emotional security and 4) a low level of anxiety.

THE INTEGRATING FORCES IN PERSONALITY DEVELOPMENT

We are now in a position to list the integrating forces which draw people together into interpersonal relationships. The first of them occurs in infancy and the last in adolescence. Those which begin in the juvenile period and adolescence continue to exercise a strong force on interpersonal relationships during the rest of the person's life. We shall consider these integrating forces under the headings of the various periods of personality development—infancy, childhood, the juvenile period and adolescence—and in doing so shall present a brief recapitulation of personality evolution and indicate how the integrating forces bind it into a cohesive whole.

Infancy

1) The first integrating force is *the infant's need for close contacts with persons to meet his biological requirements* for food, warmth, cleanliness and other physiological essentials. *Linked to this is a strong need for affectionate physical interactions with persons who, by their attitudes and feelings, transmit the feeling that he is a valued person.* This need is, of course, primarily met in the mother-child relationship, but it can be equally satisfied in warm relationships with any or all individuals who assume the mother's role.

2) The next integrating force is *tenderness,* a word Sullivan employs as a technical term. Tenderness embraces *all the anxiety-free, affectionate things that go on between the mother and the infant.* It is an interpersonal force that does not exist solely in the mother or the child, but is composed of feelings and reactions of each one that criss-cross in the interpersonal field between them.

Childhood

3) During late infancy and throughout childhood (childhood is here defined as extending from about the age of one and a half to four years), the person has *strong needs for loving, respectful collaboration with various adults and other family members* as he slowly acquires language, toilet training and innumerable other abilities essential for interpersonal living. In these relationships, there should be little emotional pain (anxiety), and the child should develop the capacity for comfortable *consensual validation.*

Juvenile Period

4) During the juvenile years, roughly from the age of four through 11 or 12, the individual has *an urgent need for vibrant relationships with nonfamily children of his own age group.* In these expanding circles of activity, he achieves new interpersonal skills, such as those for comfortable collaboration, competition and compromise. He also has, for the first time, opportunities *in nonfamilial settings* to correct personality problems through close association and consensual validation with new people.

5) At this time he experiences concomitant *needs for acceptance by nonfamily children and adults as a worthwhile, esteemed person. Loneliness* and the threat of *ostracism* (words which have special connotations in Sullivan's scheme of development) are spurs to his integration in broader interpersonal situations.

6) In the last phase of the juvenile period, which Sullivan separates off as *preadolescence* and which varies from a few months to two or three years in length, a person has *a need for a particularly close relationship with a friend of the same sex.* In this relationship, which should be free of any genital sexual activity, the individual first experiences *intimacy,* which occurs when another person's well-being means as much to a person as his own welfare. In sharing ongoing and past experiences, in both verbal and nonverbal ways, this intimate relationship offers a person further chances for sound consensual validations, the correction of parataxic distortions and added emotional growth.

Many commentators on Sullivan's works feel that in most people true intimacy first occurs in early or middle adolescence, and in his final years Sullivan seemed to be inclining toward this point of view.

Adolescence

7) Adolescence ushers in the last integrating force, *lust. Here a person is integrated in close relationships with persons of the opposite sex, in which genital sexual activity is an immediate or distant, possible goal.* The union of lust and intimacy forms a drive of special strength which continues through most of the rest of life.

The person who fails to achieve reasonable satisfaction of any of the needs produced by these integrating forces is prone to interpersonal maladjustments. His repertory of modes of experience is limited or distorted. Marked limitations or distortions may lead to the kinds of personality malformations, and other types of difficulty, which are labeled psychiatric illness.

THE CONCEPT OF DYNAMISMS IN ADOLESCENCE
AND OTHER LIFE PERIODS

Dynamisms form a central concept in Sullivan's system of personality development. Though they begin to operate in infancy and childhood, they achieve their full-fledged development during adolescence; from then on they have profound effects on the individual's interpersonal functioning.

Early in his psychiatric career Sullivan noted that many concepts in diverse schools of psychiatry are based on metaphors adopted from Newton's system of mechanics. They portray emotional functioning in terms of forces operating against each other, opposing or balanced weights, vector arrows that penetrate or are blocked by barriers, spaces that may be invaded or may repel impinging forces, and many other mechanical devices. He felt that such metaphors were poor ways for representing emotional suffering. He also pointed out that there is no way for scientifically proving which, if any, of the competing systems employing such concepts are valid.

Sullivan therefore abandoned all such conceptions and developed the concept of dynamisms. *A dynamism is a relatively enduring pattern of energy transformation which characterizes the emotional functioning and interpersonal relationships of a person.*

Dynamisms deal with the transformation and flow of energy, and human beings are constantly transforming energy; as we shall see, each feeling, thought and interpersonal event requires the transformation and flow of a great deal of energy in diverse ways. Concepts of emotional functioning based on mechanical models can never be anything more than fanciful metaphors, whereas energy transformation and flow is what actually occurs in people.

Energy transformations and flow are more difficult to understand than mechanical movements. Most people can comprehend more easily the motions of weights and pulleys, and diagrams similar to geographical maps, than they can grasp the principles of energy transformation. Hence, acceptance of Sullivan's concept of dynamisms has been slow and it often has been misunderstood.

A dynamism is best understood by 1) identifying the source of its energy, and 2) tracing the course of its energy transformations and flows until it finds final expression in an interpersonal event.

The *source* of a dynamism in many cases lies in biochemical and biophysical processes in a person, though in some instances it is interpersonal in origin; this will be made clear later on in this section. Its *course* consists of energy transformations and flows in the person which lead to events in his relationships with one or more people.

The nature of dynamisms will be illustrated in two examples. One, for the sake of simplicity, will be taken from infancy. The other, though still somewhat simplified, will involve more complex activities of adolescents.

A four-month-old infant experiences the discomfort which in later years he will know as hunger. This sensation is produced by contractions of his stomach and intestines, changes in his blood sugar level and many other biochemical and biophysical factors. This is the *source* of the energy of his dynamism.

Energy transformations and flows begin as he cries, moves his arms and legs and in other ways indicates his uneasiness. This brings his mother to him with a bottle of milk; she cuddles him and talks to him as she feeds him. The feelings, thoughts and physical actions of the mother and the child require vast numbers of complex transformations and flows of energy in nervous, hormonal, muscular, emotional and interpersonal ways. These constitute the *course* of the dynamism. *The dynamism finds its final expression in an interpersonal event, the nursing of the child by his mother.* Moreover, this dynamism is *characteristic* of the mother and the child, since the mother-child relationship is sound. If, in contrast, the mother were rejecting and hostile to the infant, and the infant as a result whimpered lowly or thrashed in howling rage when hungry, the *characteristic* flow of energy of the dynamism would be quite different.

The second illustration of dynamisms involves adolescents. An 18-year-old woman sits next to an 18-year-old man in a college class. Intricate hormonal and central nervous system factors in each of them create levels of sexual interest and tension which cause them to become friends, to date and in time to have sexual intercourse. The *source* of the dynamism lies in biochemical and biophysical forces in each of them, and the *course* of the dynamism leads through physical states of sexual interest and arousal into socially acceptable ways of relating to each other and becoming sexually united. In this illustration a great deal of material is condensed into few sentences for the sake of clearness, since our aim is not to discuss the interpersonal activities of these two persons but to outline the nature of a dynamism.

This dynamism is *characteristic* of the 18-year-old woman and the 18-year-old man. It is molded by all the significant interpersonal things that have happened to them throughout their lives. If the woman's life experience (we are viewing this dynamism from her point of view rather than the man's) had been different, her *characteristic* dynamism might have been different. She might have had a homosexual relationship with the woman sitting on her left rather than a heterosexual one with the man sitting on her right. If she had been reared in a strict religious sect that stressed premarital chastity, she might have stopped short of genital sexual activity. If she had been subjected to much interpersonal trauma during her formative years, she might have become anxious, or even panic-ridden, about becoming close to the man, and she might have fled any efforts he made to get to know her well. In each case the flows of energy in the emotional and interpersonal phases of the dynamism would have been *characteristic* of her general pattern of interpersonal life.

Dynamisms, along with such processes as security operations and parataxic distortions, to a large extent distinguish a person as the individual whom we know. When we say that Susan is shy with men, or is hostile toward them, or gets along well with them, we are describing in colloquial terms one of her *characteristic dynamisms*. Mental health professional workers do the same thing, but they do it in much more detail and depth, and they use more precise language.

A dynamism is a comprehensive process. It often embraces security operations, patterns for meeting needs, customary ways of relating to people, parataxic distortions and other emotional and interpersonal functions which characterize the person. For example, if the 18-year-old woman described above had bickered with the man to avoid becoming truly close to him she 1) would have been avoiding the anxiety of a close heterosexual contact by means of an unhealthy security operation and thus 2) would have been revealing a significant segment of her self-system (that is, the sum of all her security operations). She also 3) would have been carrying out a parataxic distortion which was the product of unhealthy interpersonal relationships with important persons in her earlier years. Other processes would have entered into her dynamism, but we are listing only three of them as we indicate the all-embracing nature of a dynamism.

The concept of a dynamism thus unites many functions which are fragmented in other psychiatric systems. For example, it embraces the forces and operations which are termed instincts, drives, libido, love objects, cathexes, defense mechanisms and others. Hence, it stresses the unity of emotional and interpersonal functioning in each thing a person feels, thinks and does.

As indicated briefly at the beginning of this discussion, in order to cover all aspects of living, the concept of the *source* of energy in a dynamism must be broadened to include interpersonal sources. That is, the source of the energy may be the turbulence generated by traumatic interpersonal events and relationships. A much simplified illustration makes this clear. Throughout his life an adolescent has been reared in a hostile, depreciating, rejecting environment and emerges from his formative years with profound feelings of personal worthlessness. At 16 he experiences an abrupt, harsh rejection by a girl friend. This sets in motion a dynamism in which he becomes depressed, apathetic and withdrawn from people for a period of several weeks. This is the *relatively enduring pattern of energy transformation which characterizes his emotional functioning and interpersonal relationships when he is confronted with this kind of situation.* The source of the energy which sets this dynamism in motion is interpersonal; it lies in interpersonal turbulence generated by a traumatic upbringing and a disturbing interpersonal event. From middle adolescence onward, the sources of energy in dynamisms tend to be interpersonal.

However, an interpersonal source of energy in a dynamism is, in the final analysis, biochemical and biophysical. Each feeling, thought and action of the 16-year-old boy described above can occur only by virtue of large numbers of complex biochemical and biophysical events in his central nervous system and other body organs. Vast numbers of sodium and potassium ions crisscross semipermeable membranes of nerve fibers as waves of depolarization and polarization course along them, and hormonal, muscular and other organic reactions must transpire if this dynamism is to occur. Hence, when we say that the source of energy in a dynamism is emotional and interpersonal we are merely describing it from an interpersonal point of view. This in no way minimizes the role of emotional and interpersonal events in personality functioning and in dynamisms; it merely makes the concept of dynamisms more comprehensive.

Dynamisms may be healthy or unhealthy. Thus, Sullivan sometimes speaks of the obsessional dynamism in discussing obsessive-compulsive disorders and the paranoid dynamism in writing on paranoid difficulties. As will be discussed in Chapter 7, much of the work done in psychotherapy consists of unraveling dynamisms which are causing patients difficulties in living.

PERSONALITY PROBLEMS IN ADOLESCENCE

During adolescence various kinds of maladjustments may occur as a person struggles to find expression for his needs for *emotional security, intimacy* and *lust.* Lust puts an added strain on the individual's needs for sound, intimate relationships; in many cases they must be modified to accommodate the added dimension of genital sexuality.

For example, a person who has been able, despite personality limitations, to make reasonable adjustments with his peers and with adults during the juvenile period may experience much emotional discomfort when lust drives him or her toward close relationships with people of the opposite sex. In some cases the person may be unable to adjust comfortably to this added feature of interpersonal life; strong anxiety, or even panic, may occur. A flight from close relationships of all kinds occurs in a few individuals, producing schizoid or frankly schizophrenic pictures. In some instances the drives for lust and intimacy can be combined only in relationships with persons of the same sex. Many security operations and parataxic distortions which so far had caused little interpersonal trouble become the sources of major problems during adolescence. For these reasons, the incidence of various kinds of neurotic disturbances, such as obsessive-compulsive problems and hysterical disorders, rises sharply during adolescence. Psychotic disorders which are relatively uncommon in children and juveniles, such as schizophrenia and severe depressions, increase markedly during the adolescent years.

The intense emotional involvement and surrender of himself required in a relationship in which intimacy and lust are combined may menace a person's feelings of self-esteem and interpersonal competence. Lust, the last of the integrating forces that draw people together in interpersonal relationships, puts all prior integrating forces under a new strain. Thus, a person's needs for tenderness, for consensual validation and respectful collaboration with others, for vibrant relationships with people in a wide range of interpersonal settings and for protection against loneliness and ostracism are all subjected to new tensions when they must be interwoven with lust.

At this point Sullivan discusses masturbation as a *noninterpersonal* way for expressing lust. Masturbation gives expression in a solitary manner to an integrating force which should be drawing a person into a close, significant relationship. Sullivan, writing in the 1920s and 1930s, protested against society's censure of any genital-to-genital, interpersonal expression of lust for a number of years after it developed, and saw masturbation to a large extent as the noninterpersonal result. Attitudes about sexual activity have, of course, changed much in the half century since he expressed these views, but his point still retains much validity.

The ways in which parataxic distortions may be exacerbated by lust are numerous. For example, a girl who had a harsh, hostility-laden relationship with her father throughout her formative years and who hence tends to rebel against men may adjust without too much difficulty throughout her juvenile years. However, she has marked problems in her relationships with men when lust forces her into close, collaborative relationships with them.

In a similar manner, lust may cause security operations which formerly caused little interpersonal difficulty to become major problems in adolescence. Thus, selective inattention, a security operation discussed in Chapter 3, often causes much more constriction of an individual's field of awareness during adolescence than in childhood and the juvenile period owing to the pressures that lust creates. For example, a late adolescent man selectively inattends many interpersonally difficult qualities of a woman with whom he forms an intimate, lustful relationship. His strong needs for the intimate, lustful relationship cause him to selectively inattend all the things that would impair the relationship or break it up. Similarly, a girl who finds closeness with men threatening may selectively inattend desirable features of a man toward whom lust draws her, and she includes in her focus of awareness only those personality characteristics which tend to destroy closeness with him.

Lust increases selective inattention in numerous interpersonal relationships which are not primarily lustful, but might become tinged by it. Hence, a person's needs for tenderness, affectionate collaboration and consensual validation in many kinds of interpersonal settings, such as vocational and social ones, may be unfulfilled because of increasing selective inattention; the person shuns relationships in which lust is not the main integrating force but only a remotely possible intruder.

This is, incidentally, one of the reasons why children and juveniles often are more perceptive of the true feelings and attitudes of people than adolescents and adults are. Children and juveniles cannot crystallize their perceptions in words as well as older persons can, but their awareness of how people feel about them is less constricted by the selective inattention that lust promotes.

ADEQUATE ADULTHOOD

With the development of lust, the last of the major integrating forces, and the assumption of the repertory of vocational, economic and interpersonal responsibilities that characterize adulthood, a person in his early twenties is ushered into full adult status.

Personality never becomes rigid and fixed. Throughout life, in small or large ways, an individual's associations with people continue to change, and his characteristics of living and experiencing are subject to constant alterations. Nevertheless, the broad personality patterns laid down in the first two decades of life have strong tendencies to persist.

Sullivan rarely uses the word maturity; it is difficult to define, and also encourages the employment of its counterpart, immaturity; this latter term has in some circles acquired a disparaging connotation. Instead, he speaks of *adequate adulthood*, or *interpersonally adequate adulthood*.

A person with adequate adulthood has had healthy satisfaction of his needs for close relationships with people in infancy, childhood, the juvenile period and early and late adolescence. The main integrating forces characterizing each period have resulted in sound relationships with the persons who were at that time important. His level of anxiety is low most of the time and his security operations are for the most part healthy; this is another way of saying that his abilities for coping with interpersonal challenges are good. His self-system, embracing his various security operations, functions well in keeping him in a state of emotional comfort most of the time. He has well developed capacities for consensual validation on both superficial and profound matters. He has secure self-esteem and treats others with sound respect. Whatever parataxic distortions he has are minor and cause him no significant difficulties in living. All these things operate in contexts of healthy interpersonal relationships.

An adequate adult has comfortable ways of satisfying his needs for giving and receiving tenderness, for collaborating with people in both trivial and important activities and for avoiding the pain of loneliness and ostracism. He has sound capacities for expressing his needs for intimacy and lust, and can combine these two needs in long-term, gratifying living with another person.

His field of awareness is relatively broad, and he can bring into the focus of his awareness the feelings, thoughts and experiences which he needs in making the manifold adjustments he must make each day. His interpersonal life widens steadily, or at least his ongoing interpersonal associations maintain their energy and vitality, and he has the kinds of experiences which give meaning and significance to what he is doing with his life.

Adequate adulthood is obviously a galloping goal. It is not a fixed point at which a person arrives. This makes life a continual challenge as each individual faces new interpersonal situations and changing circumstances.

Chapter 7

The Therapeutic Implications of Sullivan's Concepts of the Juvenile Period and Adolescence

AWARENESS AND UNAWARENESS IN PSYCHOTHERAPY

One of the basic aims of therapy is to enable a person to include many more of his feelings and thoughts, and various aspects of his interpersonal relationships, in his field of awareness. During therapy things that previously were too painful for awareness become incorporated into his fund of assimilated, articulate experience. By such expansion of his awareness, he is freed to enter new kinds of interpersonal activity, which in turn has healthy effects. Emotional growth thus generates more emotional growth.

Sullivan states that a person is emotionally healthy to the extent that he or she is aware of the nature and meaning of his interpersonal experience. This includes both his ongoing and past experience. By awareness Sullivan does not mean a cold, mechanical knowledge of what is going on and has gone on in a person's life. He means a profound assimilation of feelings, thoughts and experience which is gained gradually as the therapist and the patient repeatedly examine, from various points of view, diverse aspects of the patient's interpersonal life. The patient's newly gained awareness is further explored as he

90

carries it into the current relationships of his life. Each new insight gained about his past interpersonal life is examined in terms of its impact on his current interactions with people. *Therapy is an expansion of experience through awareness.*

For example, in therapy a withdrawn, schizoid person slowly achieves awareness that his upbringing by depreciating, rejecting parents left him with feelings of low self-esteem and personal worthlessness. Such awareness about his *past* is then examined in terms of how it affects his various *present* interpersonal relationships. He gradually becomes aware that in each current relationship he feels that when another person gets to know him well that person will abandon him in disgust as a worthless, inadequate individual. Exploration of a number of ongoing relationships—with school acquaintances, with girl friends and with others—in time reveals that such abandonment does not occur. As months, or perhaps years, pass, his self-esteem rises as he becomes aware of how *past* relationships create anxieties that hamper *present* associations with people. *Awareness frees him for new kinds of interpersonal experience, and this experience modifies his view of himself and his capacities for interactions with people.* This much simplified case vignette illustrates how awareness of past and present relationships is woven into a single fabric in interpersonal psychotherapy.

The concepts of *covert* and *overt* experience, as discussed in Chapter 1, have extensive implications for the kinds of therapy that can be done with children, as opposed to that which can be done with adolescents. A covert experience is one which cannot be talked over, neither when it occurs nor at a later time; almost all experiences of infancy, and many of those of early childhood, are covert. They can be observed, as in observation of an infant during feeding or a young child in interaction with its mother, but neither at the time of its occurrence nor in later years can either experience be discussed with a therapist to help the person expand his awareness. Consensual validation of this material is not possible. Treatment of emerging emotional problems in infants and children must therefore be carried out by play therapy, in which nonverbal factors and the child-therapist relationship are important, and interview work with parents helps them change their attitudes toward the infant or child and achieve new ways of interacting with him. This, of course, constitutes the child guidance clinic approach or some modification of it.

Sullivan stresses that once the individual arrives at the juvenile period of mental health professional is on somewhat surer ground, both scientifically and therapeutically, in terms of what the person is experiencing. The patient has developed the language capacities and other techniques for much advanced communication, both verbally and nonverbally. The possibilities for consensual validation with a skilled participant observer are much greater. This profoundly affects the therapist's techniques for expanding the patient's awareness.

In therapeutic terms, the juvenile period is a middle ground. Whether the therapist uses play therapy and depends heavily on a nonverbalized constructive relationship with the patient, or whether he employs a certain amount of interview work to explore the patient's current and past experience, varies much from case to case. In general, there is more reliance on the former than the latter. Awareness is expanded only in simple ways in dealing with a juvenile patient, and consensual validation is sought on only a few fundamental things such as basic feelings, marked anxieties and low self-esteem. Much emphasis is placed on increasing the awareness of the parents in interviews with them about how their unhealthy interactions with the juvenile may be improved.

In adolescence the balance shifts rapidly toward broad-ranging interview work with the patient, using all the special techniques for talking with a teenager on his own level. Consensual validation and the expansion of awareness, in language familiar to the adolescent and to the extent that he can tolerate it, become the major avenues of therapy. In other words, the patient's shift from *covert* experience to *overt* experience has moved therapy much closer to the model of adult psychotherapy. In late adolescence therapy often is directed toward an expansion of awareness similar to that sought in therapy with adults.

Though the aims of therapy in middle and late adolescence are expansion of awareness and consensual validation, there are particular problems which require special techniques and cautions. The adolescent often has much anxiety which tends to block therapy. He is struggling to combine lust harmoniously with all his other integrating forces, and he is trying to reach a comfortable adjustment in a steadily expanding interpersonal world which demands much more self-reliance and achievement from him. Special sensitivity to the adolescent's abrupt rises in anxiety is needed if maximum awareness is to be reached.

THE EXPLORATION OF DYNAMISMS

A psychotherapist spends a great deal of his time studying dynamisms, the relatively enduring patterns of energy transformation which characterize the emotional functioning and interpersonal relationships of a person. He traces 1) the source of each dynamism's energy, 2) the transformations and flow of its energy in the individual's feelings, thoughts and actions and 3) the final expression of the energy in one or more interpersonal events. Psychotherapeutic work rarely proceeds in so systematic a manner as this outline suggests, but this format gives order and direction to the therapist's understanding of the patient as he discusses his life in wide-ranging ways.

Therapy usually begins with past or present interpersonal incidents, which may or may not appear to be relevant to the patient's presenting problems. It then works backward over the complex course of the energy flow which has found expression in interpersonal events; the source, especially if it it is interpersonal, is in many cases the last area to be explored. Several areas may be under consideration at the same time, and their close or loose relationship to each other may not be clear at first. In the exploration of dynamisms the only absolute rule is the absence of all rules except alert flexibility. Abrupt rises in the patient's anxiety, unexpected bursts of insight through consensual validation and unforeseen openings of fresh areas for investigation determine the paths an interview, or a series of interviews, takes. In some cases the source of a dynamism's energy is first exposed, and only later are its courses and interpersonal consequences examined.

The following case vignette, much simplified to indicate clearly the exploration of a dynamism in psychotherapy, is drawn from our patient files. Moreover, the sequence of events in this course of psychotherapy was not as systematic as the vignette suggests; areas of the patient's life were repeatedly approached from varying points of view, with other material frequently interspersed, as consensual validation was slowly reached on things often summarized here in one or two sentences.

Interpersonal Events. The interpersonal events produced by this dynamism will be presented first since interpersonal disturbances usually are the things which draw a patient to the attention of a psychiatrist or other mental health professional. The source of the dynamism and the course of its various transformations and flows of energy became apparent only as therapy proceeded.

A 22-year-old man, attending college in a city distant from that in which his parents lived, underwent a marked change in his interpersonal life during a several-day period. He withdrew from people and viewed them at times with apprehensive suspiciousness. His uneasiness increased rapidly until he was interpersonally paralyzed in an acute panic state. He huddled in his room and stared wildly about, answering questions in monosyllables and waving aside all offers of help. Prior to this abrupt change he had been a somewhat shy, tense person, but he had adjusted in a seemingly adequate manner.

Source. The source of the energy of this dynamism lay in both his formative years and in recent and ongoing events.

He had been reared by a domineering, cold father and a floundering, demanding mother. Each parent used him as a weapon against the other in their chronic marital difficulties; each parent played him off against the other one, and attributed any shortcomings the patient had to the other parent's handling of him. His father used depreciating harangues to dominate him and his mother employed guilt-laden tirades to manipulate him. This behavior was made all the more traumatic by their indulgent behavior toward his older brother.

The smoldering resentment, low self-esteem, marked guilt feelings and confused anguish which his childhood years generated in him constituted an important source of energy in his dynamism.

When he was 18, this man left his parent's home for the first time to attend college in a distant city. During his four years of college he spent his summers traveling with college friends or on extended field trips connected with his studies. For the first time, divorced from environments dominated by his parents or chosen by them, he found interpersonal relationships in which he was treated as a worthwhile, able, esteemed person. He had previously felt, in ways of which he was only dimly aware, that all close associations with people were painful traps and that cautious noninvolvement was the only manner in which a tolerable life pattern could be achieved. In his four college years he developed new, but as yet unconsolidated, capacities for making emotional investments in people. He was in the process of experimenting with interpersonal commitments combining intimacy and lust when his progress was shattered.

Three months before graduation, after which he was scheduled to go to graduate school, his father was partially incapacitated by a ruptured intracranial aneurysm. Both parents, who had mainly ignored him since he had gone away to college, began to harangue him to return home after graduation to assume responsibilities in the family business. This would have involved working closely with both his parents in the business. By letters and long distance telephone calls, his parents alternated between sobbing appeals and guilt-laden tirades to get him to come home.

Thus, his painful interpersonal past threatened to engulf him once more, and the four constructive, comfortable years he had known at college, and the healthier way of life he was achieving, seemed to be slipping away from him. Tortured by feelings of guilt, unworthiness and impotent rage, he felt unable to resist his parents' appeals. The emotional turbulence of this situation provided the second source of energy which set his dynamism in motion.

Course. The clinical picture of this patient might be termed a severe panic state or an incipient schizophrenic reaction. In it the emotional turmoil generated both in the traumatic relationships of his formative years and in his current interpersonal crisis produced feelings of terror, helplessness and self-loathing; his self-esteem deteriorated and he was flooded with panic. The transformations and flows of energy involved in these processes profoundly altered his interpersonal feelings, thoughts and actions. He retreated from all interpersonal contacts, for they signified only suffering and exploitation to him. This withdrawal also prevented a return to the intolerable emotional environment of his childhood and early adolescence.

This dynamism operated largely outside the patient's field of awareness. He could grasp only that some hideous emotional and interpersonal calamity had befallen him, but he had no more than vague, fragmentary conceptions of its causes and the ways in which it was operating in his life.

Emotional and interpersonal forces were interlocked in this flow of energy. Terror produced withdrawal, and withdrawal reduced the pressures which were producing the terror.

Therapy involved the slow exploration of the interpersonal *sources* of his anguish and its intricate *course* toward isolation and incapacitation. This was done during an initial period of hospitalization in which phenothiazine medication was utilized to help assuage his panic and thus facilitate interpersonal treatment, and this exploration continued during a year of outpatient psychotherapy sessions two or three times a week. At first, therapy dealt only with his feelings of worthlessness and inadequacy as a person. The main work of tracing his dynamism from its sources to its interpersonal consequences was carried out as stepwise reduction of his panic and lesser anxiety permitted it. In this process he grew emotionally and was, in time, able to establish a life independent of his parents. He was able once more to begin to form nonfamily relationships involving close collaboration with others, intimacy and lust.

Few cases seen in actual practice are as clear-cut as this one was; it was because of the clearness with which it could be outlined in such little space that it was chosen to illustrate how therapists deal with dynamisms.

Two Further Aspects of the Therapeutic Use of Dynamisms. Firstly, when a therapist is employing Sullivan's concept of dynamisms, he is using the basic twentieth century approach to science. In the nineteenth century most models in physical, biological and psychological fields were based on Newton's system of mechanics. Scientific workers in the twentieth century tend to see all activities, both in living and inanimate processes, in terms of transformations and flows of energy. The concepts of Einstein, Planck and many others in the physical sciences, and of most investigators in biological fields, are focused on how energy is transmitted. Sullivan was aware of this. In this connection he cited the work of Alfred North Whitehead, the scientist and philosopher who was Bertrand Russell's collaborator in much of Russell's early work. So far as we know, Sullivan's approach to psychology and psychiatry is the only one that is in keeping with this marked reorientation in scientific thinking that began in the early years of this century. In our opinion, this gives interpersonal psychotherapy a special cogency.

Secondly, Sullivan's term dynamism tends to be confused by mental health professional workers with the terms dynamics and psychodynamics. An unwary reader of Sullivan's works may not understand that he is talking about something much more specific than these two general terms connote. This confusion has retarded the diffusion of Sullivan's concept of dynamisms.

THE PRINCIPLE OF RECIPROCAL EMOTIONS IN THE THERAPEUTIC RELATIONSHIP

Sullivan gives much attention to how the principle of reciprocal emotions operates in the patient-therapist relationship. He points out that both the patient and the therapist have needs, patterns of interaction and future expectations about what is going on in each therapeutic session.

Difficulties arise when an inexperienced therapist is *unaware* of how his needs, patterns of interaction and expectations may be influencing treatment. The following example illustrates the operation of the principle of reciprocal emotions in such a situation.

An adult patient, consulting a therapist for the first time, *needs* help for his anxiety states and concomitant obsessive thoughts. The therapist *needs* to feel that he is a competent professional person who possibly can aid the patient; without such a need he could hardly undertake in good faith the task which the patient presents to him. A novice in therapy also may have *needs* for the patient to discuss the kinds of things which support the therapist's viewpoints about the causes of anxiety states and obsessive-compulsive problems.

Out of these needs, *interpersonal patterns* are set up between the therapist and the patient; in this case, for purposes of illustration, the therapist is not aware of how the principle of reciprocal emotions is distorting the therapeutic process owing to the therapist's *unawareness* of his own needs in the therapeutic situation. When the patient meets the therapist's needs, by reporting that he is improving and by discussing the kinds of experiences which support the therapist's theories about him, the therapist subtly indicates satisfaction.

This occurs more by nonverbal than by verbal means. The tones of the therapist's voice, body postures, gestures and many other acts convey the therapist's feelings to the patient. The patient, an anxious, insecure, passive person, soon senses what kinds of things elicit from the therapist the reassurance, implied or explicit, he needs. This type of process can occur regardless of whether the therapist sits within the patient's field of vision. The therapist's general manner at the beginning and end of each session, rustling of clothing, scratching of notes, laying down and picking up a clipboard and numerous other things are easily perceptible in a silent room and make the therapist's reactions clear in his relationship with the patient.

As a result, this anxious, passive patient soon conforms to the therapist's needs, and this determines the *interpersonal patterns* that are set up in each of them. The patient reports progress and presents the material which supports the therapist's theories about him. The therapist feels that he is fulfilling his role and continues, in ways outside the awareness of both the patient and himself, to guide the course of treatment. This experience may actually be helpful to the patient, but treacherous possibilities exist since neither of the participants is aware of how the principle of reciprocal emotions is operating to meet the *needs* and set the *interpersonal patterns* of both of them. Out of these events the *future expectations* of each one are that treatment will continue in this manner until a satisfactory conclusion is reached.

Sullivan feels that the principle of reciprocal emotions, operating outside the awareness of unsuspecting therapists and patients, explains why therapists of highly divergent viewpoints can cite much case material to justify both their modes of treatment and their theories of the causes of emotional disorders. The case cited above is merely one of many ways, Sullivan says, in which much pseudotherapy can go on for long periods of time without truly dealing with the life experiences which are relevant to the patient's problems in living. Careful attention to the possible role of the principle of reciprocal emotions in therapy, using at times the collaboration of a supervising therapist, is necessary to avoid such therapeutic misadventures.

THE TENDENCY TOWARD HEALTH

In Chapter 3 one facet of Sullivan's principle of *the tendency toward health* was briefly outlined. Here we shall consider how it operates in psychotherapy.

The principle of *the tendency toward health* states that *when a person's anxieties, unhealthy security operations, unsound dynamisms, parataxic distortions and other personality difficulties are removed, or much ameliorated, in therapy, the patient spontaneously grows toward emotional and interpersonal health*. The problem in a garden, Sullivan states, is not the flowers, but the weeds; when the weeds are removed the flowers grow in healthy ways.

The tendency toward health is not a scientific principle; it is an assumption. However, there is a certain amount of general evidence to back it up. Each moment in the human body untold millions of chemical and biophysical events occur. A single thought or feeling requires that tens of millions of electrolytes crisscross the linings of millions of nerve fibers, and equally complex things are occurring at all times in every cell and organ of the body. On a statistical basis, it would seem likely that many things would go wrong in various parts of the body every minute, but they do not. Most people function reasonably well most of the time. Hence, in this aspect of human life it seems reasonable to say that there is a fundamental tendency toward health. It probably has been acquired slowly during human evolution, for anyone without it would soon become disabled.

Similarly, when all the possible anxieties, unsound security operations, defects of self-systems, unhealthy dynamisms, parataxic distortions and other personality problems are considered, it would seem statistically probable that most interpersonal relationships would quickly break down or generate severe conflicts. However, this does not happen. Most people get along adequately with the majority of the persons in their environments most of the time. It seems acceptable, therefore, to suggest that there is a basic tendency toward health in human emotional and interpersonal living. It presumably has been acquired over millions of years during which man gradually developed his capacities to live in interpersonal groups of continually increasing size and complexity. If this tendency toward interpersonal health had not developed, most marital, parent-child, familial, social and cultural relationships would be constantly chaotic and strife-torn.

Hence, Sullivan says, the therapist is never called upon to "cure" anyone. His job is to enter into a joint task with the patient to remove or reduce the emotional and interpersonal obstacles which are causing his troubles in living. When these are removed, the patient spontaneously grows toward emotional and interpersonal soundness. In a sense, the tendency toward health makes psychotherapy and many other kinds of interpersonal mental health work in therapeutic environments feasible, for if the contrary were true, the therapeutic possibilities of psychiatric treatment would be bleak.

II

SULLIVAN'S CONCEPTS OF
PSYCHIATRIC ILLNESS

Sullivan did not attempt to explore the interpersonal causes and treatment of all kinds of psychiatric illnesses. He limited his lectures, seminars and writings to those disorders with which he had much therapeutic experience. Thus, he lectured and wrote a great deal on schizophrenia since he had much experience in treating schizophrenics, but wrote little on manic and depressive disorders since he had little clinical experience with patients with these conditions. Such scrupulousness is uncommon among distinguished psychiatric pioneers, who often use their general theoretical formulations to speculate on the causes and treatment of psychiatric disorders with which they have had little direct contact.

In addition, Sullivan felt it was unjustified to use the outline of personality development discussed in the first half of this book to form conjectures on the origins of psychiatric illnesses he had not extensively studied in patients.

Hence, our coverage of Sullivan's concepts of psychiatric illness will be incomplete. It will deal mainly with anxiety states, panic states, obsessive-compulsive disorders, hypochondriacal conditions, hysteria, schizophrenia, paranoid states and some of the character disorders.

Chapter 8

Anxiety and Panic States

In tracing personality development in the preceding chapters, we have at various points dealt with the role anxiety (which embraces, in Sullivan's terminology, all kinds of emotional discomfort) plays in interpersonal relationships. These titers of anxiety are within normal limits. Thus, in discussing the anxiety-producing (bad) nipple, the anxiety-producing (bad) mother, the anxiety-ridden (bad) me and the panic-ridden (not) me, we have outlined things that occur in all persons in the first year of life. We have also considered how the anxiety gradient (the continually shifting balance between mild anxiety and emotional ease) has marked influences on personality development throughout the formative years and continues to be important in adult life. People are constantly modifying their relationships with others to keep their emotional discomfort, or anxiety, as low as possible. We have also noted that all anxiety is interpersonal in origin.

In this chapter we shall consider those forms of anxiety which become so marked that they cause intense discomfort and impairment in a person's interpersonal life. Such conditions are usually called acute anxiety states, chronic anxiety states and panic states, depending on their degree and duration, and they are traditionally classified among the neuroses.

103

THE INTERPERSONAL CAUSES OF ANXIETY
AND PANIC STATES

Anxiety is produced by interpersonal relationships and events that in some manner threaten the individual's integrity as a person. Anxiety-producing relationships and events menace the person's feelings of self-esteem, personal worth, adequacy and all other things that contribute to a sense of being fully human.

Thus, a mother who treats her infant with hostility, a marital partner who scornfully dominates his or her mate, and a father who harshly rejects his child are dealing with another person in ways that threaten his or her self-esteem, erode his or her feelings of worthwhileness and imply that he or she is not an adequate human being. Each interpersonal event of this kind can mobilize the many kinds of emotional anguish which are included under the broad term of anxiety.

The past history of a person to a large extent determines the kinds of interpersonal events which tend to precipitate anxiety in him. A person who was reared by rejecting, hostile parents tends to become anxious when in adolescence and adulthood someone treats him in a cold, irritable manner. A person who was reared by parents who allowed him to manipulate them by temper tantrums and sullenness tends to become anxious when in his later years he cannot dominate others by his demanding, morose behavior. The individual who emerged from his formative years with secure heterosexuality does not become disturbed when another person makes homosexual overtures to him, whereas the individual without a firm sexual orientation may become panicky when someone makes homosexual advances. In innumerable other ways, past experience makes people prone to anxiety when they encounter particular kinds of interpersonal incidents or relationships.

Anxiety often is precipitated by anticipation of what may happen in an interpersonal situation. An individual may, for various reasons, anticipate an attack on his self-esteem from a particular person, and his anxiety begins before anything traumatic actually occurs. For example, a person who was reared in a pervasively critical, depreciating environment may have an anxiety attack as he contemplates an interview with an irritable work supervisor the next day. In many instances, the anxiety-producing event may be hours, days or weeks in the future; the anxiety attack begins as the person considers what may happen when a possible situation is encountered. This frequently is the case when a patient can identify no precipitating interpersonal cause for his anxiety. He can recall only the wave of panic that passed over him and nonspecific speculations about a future event that set off the anxiety attack. In many cases the future event was dimly on the periphery of his field of awareness and not in the center of his focus of attention.

The interpersonal setting of a person's first attack of anxiety often is revealing; it may give much information about the kind of affront to his self-esteem that particularly disturbs him and the type of interpersonal relationship that is especially threatening. Such information is valuable in psychotherapy, for in future episodes of anxiety the patient may not be able to identify the incident, or the apprehensive forebodings, that caused his panic.

Sullivan feels that all anxiety is to some extent linked with the anxiety a person felt in his relationship in infancy with the anxiety-producing (bad) mother, as outlined in Chapter 1. This was his first experience with emotional discomfort, and it became the prototype for all subsequent emotional distress. Thus, whether the anxiety he experienced in this first relationship with a significant person was mild or severe, brief or prolonged, and devastating or tolerable, is of much importance.

If an individual's experience throughout infancy, and often extending into early childhood, was dominated by feelings of emotional pain and helplessness, he will be more prone to have anxiety states in his later years than if his experience in this early period was characterized by feelings of secure well-being.

Using the format of personality development in infancy outlined in Chapter 1, the individual who emerges from infancy with the concepts of the emotionally comfortable (good) me, the emotionally comfortable (good) nipple and the emotionally comfortable (good) mother as his dominant conceptions of himself and the world around him will not be prone to have anxiety and panic states in later years. In contrast, the person in whom the concepts of the anxiety-ridden (bad) me, the panic-ridden (not) me, the anxiety-producing (bad) nipple and the anxiety-producing (bad) mother are predominant will be relatively vulnerable to anxiety and panic states in subsequent years.

However, as discussed in various chapters in the first half of this book, later relationships in childhood, the juvenile period and early adolescence may extensively modify earlier forces and conceptions in healthy or unhealthy directions. A person's tendency to have anxiety states at any time in his life is affected by all his previous experience, as well as his ongoing interpersonal relationships.

Anxiety in some instances occurs when some aspect of a current interpersonal relationship threatens to bring into a person's field of awareness feelings and thoughts which are abhorrent and panic-laden for him. In an oft-cited example, this may happen when a relationship between two men, or two women, threatens to become tinged with genital homosexuality. If one of the persons has an insecure sexual orientation, and if homosexuality is a repellant thing for him, he may become acutely anxious as his homosexual urges start to invade his field of awareness. Whether or not homosexual feelings are anxiety-laden for him will, of course, depend on whether in his formative years he had the kinds of experiences which make him susceptible to this precipitant of anxiety.

Sullivan divides past experience into three broad categories, in terms of its tendencies to precipitate anxiety: 1) experience which is emotionally comfortable and easy to recall, and hence is unlikely to produce anxiety states; 2) experience which is emotionally painful and difficult to bring into awareness, and hence is somewhat prone to cause anxiety states as it impinges on the individual's field of awareness; 3) experience which is panic-laden and highly disturbing to recall, and which is therefore almost certain to precipitate an anxiety attack or frank panic when it threatens to enter the person's range of awareness or erupts into his focus of attention.

As a rule, the last two of these kinds of experience encroach on a person's field of awareness *only when ongoing interpersonal activity mobilizes them.* Something that is occurring between the person and one or more other individuals causes this past experience to hover on the person's periphery of awareness, or brings it into sharp focus; an anxiety or panic state is produced if his security operations and other personality resources cannot cope adequately with this event.

INTERPERSONAL CONSEQUENCES OF ANXIETY

Anxiety usually is a *disjunctive* (Sullivan's term) force in the interpersonal relationship that precipitates it; the relationship is emotionally painful for one or both persons, and one or both of them tend to withdraw from it. In some situations, as in marriage, recurrent anxiety may cause the relationship to terminate. In associations in which separation of the two individuals cannot occur, as in a parent-child relationship, the emotional separation is subtler; the two persons continue to live together, but meaningful communication between them decreases or ceases altogether.

In contrast, anxiety-free events are *conjunctive;* that is, they draw people together in comfortable, close relationships. Thus, anxiety states are both produced by interpersonal relationships and in turn have profound impacts on their courses.

In addition, a severe anxiety state usually impairs a person's capacity to grasp what is going on with the other person, or persons, in the relationship which provoked his anxiety. All kinds of pain hamper a person's perceptiveness of what is occurring in his environment. A person who has the abrupt onset of severe abdominal pain is less able to comprehend what is happening between him and other people. Severe anxiety operates similarly, and thus a person in an acute anxiety attack or a panic state is unable to sense what is going wrong in his interpersonal life and how it is related to past traumatic events. An anxiety state hence *constricts awareness,* and is therefore inclined to be prolonged and repeated; anxiety by its very nature robs a person of the insights he needs to correct his interpersonal life and cope with the residuals of past emotional damage.

When anxiety is mild, the upset person frequently can become aware of the things which are disturbing his relationship with another person and are producing his anxiety state. As a result, he may be able to take appropriate interpersonal steps to decrease his distress, and in the process he grows interpersonally and emotionally. The chances that he will do this are greater if he has a perceptive person to help him or professional therapeutic aid.

Some people, in time, intuitively or articulately perceive the kinds of situations that tend to produce their anxiety states, and they may become adept at avoiding them. For example, the person who becomes severely anxious in competitive settings may adjust his life to avoid such situations, and the individual who finds that close associations with persons of the opposite sex panic him avoids such relationships. However, people who arrange their activities to avoid panic-inducing relationships *do so at the cost of constricting their interpersonal lives.* Many kinds of experiences are simply cut out of their lives. If emotional health consists in being able to adjust in a wide range of situations with people, such persons are sick to the extent that their scope of experience is contracted.

We are now in a position to view the security operation of selective inattention, discussed in Chapter 3, from a broader point of view. Selective inattention operates in its most marked forms in anxiety states and panic reactions. Hence, *severe anxiety states and panic reactions, by blocking awareness of what is going on interpersonally, prevent the person from incorporating life events into his aware, assimilated experience. It is as if the events had not occurred, as far as the severely anxious or panic-ridden person is concerned. His mode of living therefore cannot improve as a result of these events and the stage is set for repeated anxiety attacks as he pushes blindly into the same kinds of settings that have mobilized emotional turmoil in him many times previously.*

Mild or moderate anxiety states occasionally have constructive results in some people. The anxiety acts as a danger sign that something is going wrong in the individual's interpersonal life. Just as the pain of a broken ankle is a warning not to walk on it, mild or moderate anxiety can alert an informed person to take stock of what is going on between himself and other people; to be helpful in this way, the degree of anxiety must be tolerable and the individual must have at least limited capacities for coping with it. In some instances, such anxiety states may motivate a person to enter psychotherapy to explore the roots of his distress.

In some persons anxiety states are the initial stages in the development of other kinds of psychiatric difficulties. They set in motion specific unhealthy security operations which decrease the person's anguish, but only at the cost of developing an obsessive-compulsive disorder, or a hysterical condition or some other neurotic process. These are considered in detail in later chapters. As we shall note later, full-fledged panic states, in a small number of cases, are the initial phases of schizophrenic illnesses.

A further complication of severe anxiety states is their tendency to create self-perpetuating vicious circles. A marital partner with acute or chronic anxiety states is a much less satisfactory person with whom to live, and his marriage deteriorates; the deteriorating marriage, in turn, adds to the interpersonal stresses that are provoking the anxiety states. An anxiety-ridden parent or child is much less gratifying than an emotionally comfortable parent or child, and the parent-child relationship worsens. Anxiety thus damages the interpersonal relationship which may be playing a role in causing it, and the total situation deteriorates.

Sullivan feels that anxiety sometimes produces hostility and outbursts of rage. The anxious person, with little or no insight into the causes of his hostility, lashes out at the person who is making him uncomfortable. By such anger, he may destroy the relationship that is producing anxiety in him, or he may modify the actions and attitudes of the person, or persons, who are distressing him. In most cases anger is unhealthy, but if the situation the angry person is destroying or modifying is sick, anger occasionally may have long-term healthy effects. In saying this, Sullivan is not advocating anger, but is merely noting one of the infrequent effects of anger when it is a product of anxiety.

DIVERSE OUTGROWTHS OF ANXIETY

Acute and chronic anxiety states may cause a wide range of emotional and physiological difficulties. The behavioral concomitants of anxiety states include alcoholism, misuse of medications and abuse of sedative or exhilarating drugs. These are all *noninterpersonal* ways of attempting to deal with interpersonally caused discomforts, and often they increase the person's underlying anxiety state by worsening his adjustments with the close people in his life. Attention may become so concentrated on the drug abuse or alcoholism that the basic anxiety state and its interpersonal causes are ignored.

Anxiety states also are causes of many of the disorders labeled psychosomatic (a term Sullivan detests). The attention of the patient and his family, and sometimes his physicians, becomes concentrated on an organic dysfunction which is merely a superficial product of interpersonal maladjustment and emotional turmoil. Sullivan discards the entire concept of psychosomatic illness and goes directly to the linkage of the particular physiological dysfunction with the things that are going wrong, or have long gone wrong, in the individual's interpersonal life. He rejects the concept of personality stereotypes for specific physical disorders in which interpersonal and emotional factors play etiological roles.

The roles of anxiety and panic states as the initial phases of some neurotic and psychotic disorders have been noted above. However, since Sullivan uses the term anxiety to embrace all forms of emotional distress, such as apprehensiveness, guilt, shame and others, this is the same things as saying that neurotic and psychotic states often pass through early stages in which the emotional suffering of the patient is naked. The obsessive-compulsive, or hysterical, or hypochondriacal, or schizophrenic, or paranoid, or other specific syndrome is a later development as the patient's emotional turmoil assumes a more elaborate form.

Sullivan, like most psychiatric writers, draws clear distinctions between anxiety and fear, and in doing so illuminates some special qualities of anxiety. Anxiety is always interpersonal in nature; it is caused by traumatic events in an individual's relationships with other people, past and present, and the person usually has little or no awareness of the true interpersonal causes of his anxiety. Fear, in contrast, is an apprehensive feeling about a real or possible danger, such as an approaching surgical operation or an oncoming automobile. Fear is not caused by past or present interpersonal truama, but by actual peril which the person faces. The person, moreover, accurately knows what he fears and can talk about it specifically.

No one ever seeks anxiety, because it is too painful and ominous, but some people find exhilaration in seeking fear by scaling mountains, riding on roller coasters and driving at high speeds. Fear is thus a much less painful experience than anxiety, and a person who courts fear feels he has reasonable control over his situation and can cope with its difficulties. A person in the throes of anxiety is in marked pain, feels helpless and feels he has no clear way of dealing with the distress which is assailing him. People rarely seek psychiatric help for fear, but anxiety is at the root of most problems for which people consult psychiatrists and other mental health professionals.

THE NATURE AND EFFECTS OF PANIC

Panic is the utmost state of terror and emotional paralysis that a person can experience. Sullivan's emphasis on panic is to a large extent based on his conviction that all schizophrenic illnesses, disorders to which he dedicated the first eight years of his psychiatric career and in which he maintained a lifelong interest, begin with brief or prolonged panic states. He feels that this period of panic is the optimum time for treating a developing schizophrenic.

Panic starts with acute *demoralization*. In Sullivan's usage, demoralization indicates a feeling by a person that he is ceasing to be fully human. His sense of integrity as a person is disintegrating and he is flooded with a feeling of impending destruction.

Two kinds of experience can produce demoralization. In the first kind, a person is subjected to severe depreciation by people who are important to him. One or more emotionally close persons treat him as a valueless object to be manipulated to gratify their convenience or malice, or they subject him to brutal rejection. This kind of demoralizing treatment usually has a long history, beginning in infancy and childhood and continuing through adolescence and adulthood into the present. Some particularly painful current incident provokes the full-blown panic state.

The second kind of experience which may produce demoralization is the eruption, or threatened eruption, of abhorrent impulses, thoughts and feelings into the person's field of awareness. For example, if incestuous feelings are stirred in an individual and hover on the periphery of his range of awareness, he may become panicky. Feelings of marked hostility, with wishes for the death of a parent or some other close person, are often cited as precipitants of panic. In each case a person's scope of awareness is menaced with the invasion of feelings and thoughts which signify to him that he is a repugnant, less than human creature.

Only a very small percentage of persons in panic states proceed into illnesses which most psychiatrists and other mental health professionals would consider schizophrenic. In the vast majority of cases the patient suffers acutely, but in time manages to mobilize his security operations and other personality resources to return to a calmer state.

A panic-ridden person is interpersonally and emotionally paralyzed. He has no capacity to see relationships between his present and past experiences and his panic. Hence, when he takes steps to end his panic, they usually are *noninterpersonal;* he seeks aid through inanimate objects such as alcohol, sedatives and illicit drugs. Frequent panic states, with lower titers of anxiety in the intervals between them, in some cases contribute to the abuse of these substances.

In panic, a person has a return of the total terror he felt in infancy during the panic-ridden (not) me experiences described in Chapter 1. All his subsequent complex interpersonal capacities collapse or are severely impaired as he retreats from the interpersonal world he has found so perilous and painful. It is a massive return to the times when everything about him seemed chaotic and menacing, and whatever he himself was seemed in dissolution.

THE THERAPY OF PANIC

A few aspects of the management of anxiety are sketched in Chapter 4 of this book and this subject is extensively discussed in our book *The Treatment Techniques of Harry Stack Sullivan*. We shall here restrict ourselves to a few general comments on the therapy of panic.

Sedative or antipsychotic medications are, of course, sometimes employed to abort a panic state and bring the patient within the sphere of a psychotherapeutic approach.

The crucial therapeutic attitude in treating panic is a profound respect for the suffering person, and this is more often transmitted nonverbally than verbally. The therapist, by his earnest concern and sincere understanding of the patient's agony, establishes a bond. In Sullivanian terms, a *conjunctive* link is forged with a patient who has lost all bridges with the interpersonal world and feels isolated in a chaotic, *disjunctive* environment. The minor things the therapist does often are more important than presumably profounder things; offering a soft drink frequently reaches the patient more effectively than offering an interpretation.

Once the patient can communicate, the therapist may state briefly what has happened to him. He may indicate that either frontal assaults on the patient's integrity as a person or seemingly loathsome forces within him have cast him into a state of terror and impotent despair. Such explanations in themselves sometimes mean little to the patient; however, he grasps that the terrifying thing that is happening to him *makes sense to someone, and that this person has much experience in dealing with such problems.* If the therapist can accomplish this he often has done all that can be done, and should be done, in the initial phase of therapy.

When the patient is hospitalized, as he often should be, the attitudes and actions of the entire therapeutic team of mental health professionals should convey the same feeling to him. Often the patient feels that he is undergoing a dissolution of personality that no one else has ever experienced. Simply comprehending that his terror is a common human experience and that professional people frequently deal with it is of much aid to him. The people caring for the patient reflect no fear or perplexity about him, but only a compassionate understanding of what he is going through. Sullivan himself had a legendary capacity for establishing contact with panic-ridden patients. He is quoted as having said, "With me there are no panicky or schizophrenic people," and numerous reports by people who saw him at work on hospital wards support his statement.

Once the patient is able to communicate more fully, and is convalescing from his panic, the therapist may cautiously begin to explore the present and past interpersonal traumas and the repellent feelings and thoughts that provoked his panic. However, such work must be done with an alert sensitivity to how much the patient can tolerate at any particular time. In many cases the most the therapist can do in early treatment is to identify the general kinds of interpersonal relationships that in some unclear manner menace the patient. In essence, he says, "We need not go into details now. They are very painful. We shall have plenty of time to look at them when it's comfortable, or at least less frightening, to do so."

Throughout his work, the therapist emphasizes that what the patient experienced was not a weird, inexplicable calamity. It was an interpersonal event, accompanied by strong emotions, and like all interpersonal occurrences it can, in time, be talked about and understood.

Chapter 9

Obsessive-Compulsive Disorders

Sullivan's concepts of the causes of obsessive-compulsive disorders are more easily understood if one first knows his views on the emotional and interpersonal functioning of adults with obsessive-compulsive disturbances. In considering these disorders we shall therefore present them first as they are seen full-blown in late adolescents and adults. We shall then trace them back to their origins in the patient's childhood years.

Sullivan usually employs the expression *obsessional* to embrace obsessive disorders, compulsive disorders and those conditions in which the patient has both obsessive and compulsive difficulties. Terminology has changed since he wrote on these dysfunctions, and we shall therefore employ the terms obsessive, compulsive and obsessive-compulsive in discussing these problems. The reader of Sullivan's works who does not understand the broad way in which he utilizes the term *obsessional* can be misled.

INTERPERSONAL AND EMOTIONAL PROCESSES IN
OBSESSIVE-COMPULSIVE PERSONS

Sullivan's views on obsessive-compulsive disorders are best approached by beginning with those obsessive states which occur in almost all persons. Almost everyone occasionally has a phrase from a popular song, or a jingle from a television program, or a lilting advertising slogan which circles obsessively in his thinking for from several hours to two or three days. A person often is annoyed by these intrusive words, but they cause him no anxiety.

Instead, they serve useful functions in many instances. The obsessive song fragment, or television jingle, or advertising slogan *helps the person prevent some painful interpersonal incident from occupying his field of awareness*. That is, so long as the song fragment or advertising slogan is occupying a large segment of his awareness, some distressing interpersonal issue is shunted out of his focus of attention.

This process is illustrated in the following simple example. A man leaves the house in the morning after an upsetting breakfast table quarrel with his wife. He turns on the car radio and hears an advertising jingle which, to his annoyance, becomes obsessively present in his thoughts for the entire morning, or the whole day. This serves a useful purpose; it prevents the disturbing breakfast table quarrel from entering his field of awareness. Without the advertising jingle constantly filling a large part of his awareness, he would ruminate about the quarrel and perhaps become angrier and more upset as he thought about it. Though the advertising jingle may be irksome, it is much less disturbing and painful than mulling over his marital argument.

Thus, when he calls his wife on the telephone at midday he talks affably with her because he has, in colloquial terms, "forgotten" their quarrel. This is merely another way of saying that it has not been in his focus of awareness because something else, the obsessive jingle, supplanted it.

The length of time the advertising jingle stays in this man's field of awareness is affected by subsequent interpersonal events. For example, if his wife calls him on the telephone during the morning and they bicker on the same subject, he may continue to have the obsessive jingle until the next day. In contrast, if he and his wife talk pleasantly on the telephone, the chances that the jingle will soon cease to preoccupy him are enhanced.

Thus, *this minor obsession is caused by interpersonal events and serves various interpersonal purposes*. It not only helps this man resolve a stressful situation with his wife, but also prevents him from being irritable with the people with whom he works and other people whom he meets during the morning; he might be sullen with them if he were mulling over his marital conflict.

This seemingly simple illustration has some far-reaching implications when it is considered carefully. It puts the entire process of obsessive-compulsive disorders exclusively on *interpersonal grounds*. It eliminates the need for speculations about processes such as the devious expression of rage, anal erotic instincts and similar things. It removes the necessity for conjectures about unobservable, unprovable processes said to be occurring in the patient's *mind,* and moves the study of obsessive compulsive difficulties to interpersonal relationships and events which are available for direct scrutiny.

Obviously, the obsessive-compulsive difficulties which bring patients to psychiatrists and other mental health workers are more complex than that outlined in this elementary example. However, the basic principle is the same.

The differences between obsessive thoughts and feelings that fall within the limits of normality and those which constitute obsessive-compulsive disorders lie in the severity and duration of the obsessive processes, the amount of emotional turmoil bound up in them, and elaborate outgrowths such as multiple obsessions and compulsive rituals.

Moreover, the obsessions in an obsessive-compulsive neurosis usually do not work smoothly. The obsessive thoughts usually are painful. For example, they may be obsessive dreads of cardiac disease or committing homicide or carrying out socially scandalous acts such as public sexual assaults. Even when they are not distressing in content, the obsessions frequently are tinged with anxiety and seem eerie and threatening to the patient; the patient with obsessive religious quandries, revolving nonsensical phrases and constant doubting often feels that his thoughts indicate impending psychosis or some other calamity. In addition, severe obsessive-compulsive conditions often persist for weeks or years, with fluctuations, and may be associated with periods of depression or acute anxiety when the obsessive-compulsive process cannot control the emotional turbulence within the patient.

OBSESSIVE-COMPULSIVE COMMUNICATION
AND VERBAL PROCESSES

We shall now proceed to discuss some of the general personality features and characteristic modes of interpersonal activity of persons with obsessive-compulsive disorders.

Sullivan points out that, if his statements are taken at face value, the obsessive-compulsive person massively miscommunicates and misinforms. To a large extent this is because he utilizes words more as tools for avoiding awareness of what is going on in his relationships with people than as means of valid communication. If asked how his marriage is, he may reply "Just fine," when actually there is much stress in it. He may say that his job is "one long series of problems" when actually it is going well. If the details of what is happening in his interpersonal settings are not carefully examined the listener is misled. However, when the listener attempts to get such details, he often must steer his way through a morass of stock words and expressions to discover the events which the obsessive-compulsive is attempting to exclude from the awareness of both himself and his companion.

The obsessive-compulsive person feels comfortable only so long as he is engaged in some kind of dialogue which is devoid of emotion and feeling. Just as the above-cited person with the minor obsession of an advertising jingle was prevented from having the emotions of his morning breakfast quarrel in his field of awareness, the obsessive-compulsive person constantly employs stereotyped statements to avoid coming to grips with his feelings about people in *all* his interpersonal events and relationships. True emotional involvement with people is continuously threatening to him.

However, the obsessive-compulsive does not miscommunicate and mislead when he is talking about things unrelated to his relationships with people. If he is explaining the components of a machine or describing a new bookkeeping system he usually communicates well. In fact, his precise, meticulous use of words may make him superior in such tasks. Having, as it were, become an expert in employing words to keep the significance of his interpersonal relationships out of his field of awareness, he can utilize the same expertise when he deals with things that are not interpersonal.

As will be outlined more fully in a later section, these verbal characteristics of an obsessive-compulsive individual have their origins in severe parataxic distortions which he carried out of infancy, childhood and the juvenile period. However, whereas most persons with parataxic warps have difficulties only in certain kinds of situations, the obsessive-compulsive *continually* is behaving parataxically with *all* people, and in doing so he uses defective communication to avoid close contacts with them. That is, he is treating other people as if they were one or more close persons from his childhood with whom he had painful relationships. In these painful relationships he evolved elaborate, misguiding word usage to keep anxiety-laden things out of his focus of awareness, and he continues in this entrenched pattern in all his adolescent and adult relationships.

An elementary example illustrates this. A girl had harsh relationships with her parents and other close persons throughout her developing years and developed obsessive-compulsive language usage to hide from herself awareness of the hostility she expects in all subsequent settings. By treating all later persons as if they were her parents, she is carrying her parataxic warp into all aspects of her interpersonal life, and with it the obsessive-compulsive use of language which constricts awareness and makes her life tolerable.

This is in marked contrast to what happens in most other kinds of disorders in which parataxic distortions play roles. In other disorders, the parataxic distortion is restricted to some specific sphere of interpersonal activity. For example, a boy with a brutal, rejecting father rebels in adolescence and adulthood against any male authority set over him, but gets along reasonably well with all other persons with whom he has dealings; his parataxic distortion is thus restricted to a particular kind of situation.

To recapitulate, the obsessive-compulsive uses massive miscommunication as a protective device in a diffuse parataxic distortion that affects every interpersonal relationship he has, whereas persons with most other kinds of parataxic difficulties have them only in special kinds of relationships. The ways in which these other parataxic distortions manifest themselves are, in addition, different from those which characterize the obsessive-compulsive.

This feature of the compulsive person gives him characteristics that are apparent quickly to the clinical eye when he enters psychotherapy. Whereas a patient who rebels against all authoritative figures often does not begin to be hostile toward the therapist until he has been in therapy for at least a short time, the obsessive patient reveals his parataxic warp from the first moment he is seen. His frigid, mechanical use of words, his tendency to speak of all his relationships in stereotyped molds, the physical precision of his body movements and many other things are quickly apparent to the experienced therapist. The parataxic process is a barrier between the two of them from the minute therapy begins.

INTERPERSONAL CONSEQUENCES OF
OBSESSIVE-COMPULSIVE STATES

The obsessive-compulsive's urgent need to keep everything on the level of its strict verbal meaning, and to avoid awareness of feelings and expression of them, has various results. Words are stripped of their emotional content and the acts they indicate are carried out in unfeeling ways. For him "love" means the meticulous fulfillment of marital or parental obligations; his acts of "love" are devoid of tenderness and sensitivity. He behaves with brisk directness and even crudeness in many acts that should be tender and considerate. In sexual intercourse, for instance, he often behaves with an impulsive coarseness that is devoid of sensitive collaboration.

As a result of these qualities the obsessive-compulsive person often causes perplexity and distress in those who try to be close to him. People try in vain to secure his affection, only to find a coldness and insensitivity which they cannot understand and which they feel may be owing to failings in themselves. Thus, in many cases an obsessive-compulsive causes a good deal of suffering to his marital partner, children and other near persons. All may coast along in a mechanically smooth but unfeeling way as long as these persons remain convenient objects in his life. However, if people push too hard to become close to him or to modify his behavior they precipitate much anxiety, or flight or irritability.

An obsessive-compulsive individual may have a meticulous glibness which acts as a further barrier against closeness to people. He covers subjects point by point in a methodical way, as if he were delivering a lecture instead of talking with his marital partner, or children, or work associates or others. He talks about both trivia and important things in a flat, emotionless way; his speech lacks fluctuations of voice tone and emotional coloring. At times he speaks in a rapid flow which prevents responses from the person to whom he is talking, and he neither comes to a conclusion nor allows the other person to do so. In brief, he is using talk to prevent involvement with the other person. Nevertheless, he does not allow his hearer to get away, but grapples him with a monologue that permits neither true communication nor termination of the conversation. Sullivan at times refers to this as the "stickiness" or "flypaper quality" of obsessive-compulsive persons.

The talk and acts of an obsessive-compulsive often exasperate other people, for they feel impotent to make contact with him; they are perplexed that despite his garrulousness no communication is going on. They feel that something is lacking in the relationship, but they cannot discover what it is.

In many cases the obsessive-compulsive person is coldly argumentative; he must drive on in a conversation until he wins his point or coerces his companion to do as he wishes. As we shall see when we discuss the causes of obsessive-compulsive disorders, he cannot stand to be wrong. His low self-esteem and underlying feelings of worthlessness push him constantly to demonstrate that he is right on all points. He feels that he must not lose power over the circumstances and people with whom he is dealing, for if he does he will be swamped by the situation, and his self-esteem (that is, his feelings of being worthwhile as a person) will be annihilated.

An obsessive-compulsive usually has elaborate techniques for avoiding recognition of hostility both in himself and in others. If he does a punitive thing to another person, he frequently denies that there was any hostility in the act, and says in seeming justification, "It was for her own good," or "The situation required it," or "Company regulations must be carried out." Sullivan feels that this control of rage is merely one more aspect of the patient's general avoidance of open feelings. Every interpersonal relationship must be kept in apparently smooth running order. Strong feelings must be kept out of the field of awareness since they collide with the patient's basic need to maintain everything on the level of emotionless, tidy words. The camouflaging of aggressiveness and the neat control of hostility play no role in causing obsessive-compulsive difficulties; they are merely an expression of one of its many facets.

Such elaborate interpersonal and emotional operations obviously require a great deal of work, but the obsessive-compulsive as a rule shows little fatigue; on the contrary, he often has much driving energy. Sullivan speculates that during sleep much restorative activity goes on in an obsessive-compulsive individual. He, so to speak, replenishes his reserves after the constant labor during the day of maintaining the rigid structure of his obsessive-compulsive functioning. However, Sullivan emphasizes that this is only a conjecture for, as we have discussed in our book *The Treatment Techniques of Harry Stack Sullivan*, he feels there is no scientifically reliable way of examining the emotional and intellectual processes that go on during sleep. Sullivan's objections to dream analysis are complex, and discussion of them here would lead us into a long digression.

Sullivan recognizes the well known advantages sometimes inherent in a mild or moderate obsessive-compulsive disorder. By becoming absorbed with things rather than people, an individual with a mild or moderate obsessive-compulsive personality disorder may be a prodigious worker and a constructive member of a vocational group. However, the person with a severe obsessive-compulsive disorder tends to get bogged down in trivial details and is unable to work effectively. His need to get everything just right, whether it is of little or great importance, may incapacitate him in his job, his family life and in other settings.

Sullivan ignores the traditional distinction made in the official nomenclature between obsessive-compulsive personality disorders and obsessive-compulsive neuroses. In practice it is, at best, an administrative convenience, and is determined by whether the person has to a marked degree the obsessive thoughts, repetitive compulsive acts and other characteristics usually listed. Sullivan concentrates on the interpersonal life and emotional functioning of the person and considers it artificial to draw a line where obsessive-compulsive personality problems become so socially inconvenient that an obsessive-compulsive neurosis is said to exist.

THE INTERPERSONAL CAUSES OF
OBSESSIVE-COMPULSIVE STATES

During infancy, childhood and the juvenile period the obsessive-compulsive person had a brutal relationship with a close person, usually a parent. In some cases both parents were hostile, rejecting and cold. However, these persons wore masks of apparent concern and affection for the child; the child could not discern the coldness and hostility that lay behind the parental masks, or at most he had only a dim, confused perception of them.

As a result, the child felt profoundly worthless. He felt, in ways he could scarcely put into words, that he was without value and despicable. He felt that, in some manner he could not understand, he was responsible for the lovelessness, irritability and rejection that he experienced. He had no insight into the fact that these feelings were produced in him by the treatment he received from the important people around him.

To try to solve these painful interpersonal problems, the future obsessive-compulsive person begins to use words and word formulas in exaggerated ways.

At this point we must briefly consider some basic aspects of the roles of words and word formulas in interpersonal life. *Words can change the course of interpersonal incidents and relationships.* This general process is illustrated in the following example. A five-year-old child spills a glass of milk on the kitchen floor, and his mother becomes angry and scolds him. The words the child uses at this point markedly affect what happens next. If the child says, "I'm sorry. I'll clean it up," the mother becomes affectionate and says, "Well, that's all right. We all make mistakes." If, however, the child says, "It's not my fault. You filled the glass too full and made it slippery on the outside. That's why I spilled it," his mother becomes angry and a brawl between them begins. If the child says nothing at all, his mother, depending on her personality, gives him a disgusted look and mops up the milk, or rants at him and makes him feel worthless.

In each of these cases the words the child uses have a marked influence on what happens in this incident between his mother and himself, and on what occurs thereafter. Words mold interpersonal processes.

If, as in the above-cited case, traumatic incidents occur several times each day, and especially if they occur with both his parents and with other close persons, the particular words and word formulas used have strong impacts on the child's developing interpersonal relationships and concept of himself. In all these interchanges the nonverbal accompaniments of words play crucial roles; the parent's affectionate look, or angry scowl or disgusted gestures give the words added force.

The child who in later years will be obsessive-compulsive develops an excessive dependence on words as a means of trying to solve his interpersonal difficulties. He does this since he has no other way of dealing with the attitudes of others toward him and the feelings within himself. He cannot handle in an aware manner the coldness and hostility of his parents and other close persons, and he cannot otherwise come to grips with his own feelings of worthlessness and inadequacy. Words and word formulas, stripped of their emotional significance, become the only things with which he can operate in attempting to solve his own emotional pain and his problems with others.

Sullivan feels that this process is what other psychiatric writers often call the magical use of words, and that the term magic explains nothing. He feels that the interpersonal processes described above clarify why words and word formulas come to have so much importance for obsessive-compulsive people. *In this process the words and the feelings or acts become the same thing; they have the same value and significance for the child. The obsessive-compulsive evolution begins at this point.*

For example, to say, "I love you" without true feelings of affection is, for the developing obsessional child, the same thing as saying it with passion and tenderness. The child also feels that the same thing applies to his parents and others. If a parent says, "I love you" in a matter-of-fact way, for the obsessive-compulsive child it is equivalent to saying it with loving gentleness. In addition, this is true about his feelings regarding himself. If he says, either silently to himself or out loud to someone, "I feel worthwhile and able," the empty words mean the same thing as true feelings of self-esteem and adequacy, even if low self-esteem and marked feelings of inadequacy actually predominate in him. *Words disguise what actually goes on emotionally and interpersonally as the obsessive-compulsive pattern unfolds during the formative years.*

Two further things are relevant to the question why the child develops an obsessive-compulsive pattern rather than a hysterical tendency, or a hypochrondriacal inclination or some other neurotic predisposition as he struggles to solve his problems. Firstly, the masks with which the parents cover their hostility and call it "love," "responsibility," "duty" and other things seem to give words strong significance to the child; they are all he has to work with as he tries to make some sense out of what is happening between him and other people, and to achieve tolerable ease in his life.

Secondly, as we shall discuss in later sections of this chapter, obsessive-compulsive parents tend to rear obsessive-compulsive children; this is not universal, but it is frequently seen in clinical practice. Thus, the parents also tend to take words at their face values and to use words and word formulas as their principal agents in their dealings with people and their self-appraisals. Verbal interchanges take the places of emotional give-and-take. The child develops the same pattern, since in his close relationships he never encounters any other means of interpersonal living. For example, word formulas take the place of closeness to his parents, since he is exposed to no other kind of family closeness.

One of the consequences of this process is excessive conscientiousness in the child. Words such as "good," "bad" and "guilty" become highly charged. Word formulas such as "I should have done better" and "I'm sorry I did that" acquire much importance for him, both in his interpersonal associations and in his inward thoughts. These verbal devices do not solve anything, but they make the child somewhat more comfortable and smooth out his interactions with people. In addition, they decrease the emotional pain he fears from others in his interchanges with them.

The force called conscience in popular usage and theology, and superego in some psychiatric writings, is not something that is lodged in a person; *it is an interpersonal pattern, and interpersonal events mold its beginnings and its emotional concomitants.* If systematically analyzed, the feelings, thoughts and acts attributed to conscience or superego are always *interpersonal;* a person does not steal or lie because he is stealing *from someone,* or lying *to a person.* If he does not lie it is because he is trying to avoid the emotional pain which *someone threatened* if he did lie, and he dreads the implied censure of that absent person. This force is particularly stringent in the child who is forming obsessive-compulsive tendencies.

This process is enhanced in many cases by the tendencies of obsessive-compulsive parents to use moralizing sermons, as opposed to affectionate explanations, in their dealings with their children. Lacking true love and compassionate understanding, they fall back on inflexible rules of conduct in training their children in the numerous aspects of child rearing. As a result, the obsessive-compulsive child may have an excessive religiosity in his adolescence and adulthood and a wordy, hairsplitting approach to ethical behavior. The quoted rule takes the place of an affectionate feeling.

As he emerges into adolescence and adulthood, the obsessive-compulsive person's arid ways of dealing with people and feelings by verbal devices prevent him from vibrant, emotional participation with others. He therefore does not have the kinds of experiences in adolescence which might to some extent modify him by lively give-and-take with other people. If in later years he faces special interpersonal stresses, he tries to solve them by the repetitive word formulas which constitute obsessions, and the concomitant physical acts which form compulsions.

FURTHER ASPECTS OF THE DEVELOPMENT OF OBSESSIVE-COMPULSIVE STATES

Obsessive-compulsive difficulties of such proportions that they are labeled personality disorders or neuroses are occasionally seen during childhood. However, in most cases the basic pattern of obsessive-compulsive living is evolved during the formative years and, though apparent to the trained eye in childhood and the juvenile period, does not manifest itself as a full-fledged obsessive-compulsive personality disorder or neurosis until adolescence or adulthood.

A severe obsessive-compulsive neurosis is precipitated by some kind of interpersonal trauma in an adolescent or adult in whom the obsessive-compulsive way of life has been induced by childhood experiences. The interpersonal stress that provokes an obsessive-compulsive disorder is one that either assaults the individual's already low self-esteem or further undermines his feelings of inadequacy and worthlessness. In such a crisis the person attempts to deal with his emotional pain by the only techniques he has for assuaging anxiety. He uses words and word formulas in obsessive ruminations that occupy his focus of awareness most of the time and prohibit entrance of his true emotional turmoil into his field of attention. In many cases he soon develops repetitive physical acts that are the nonverbal accompaniments of his obsessive preoccupations, thus forming a fully evolved obsessive-compulsive clinical picture. As Sullivan puts it with epigrammatic simplification, the patient is kept so busy with his obsessons and compulsions that he has neither the time nor the capacity to come to grips with his real problems.

The basic interpersonal function of compulsions is similar to that of obsessions. The person who is occupied with washing his hands, or counting cracks in the sidewalk, or muttering slogans or fragments of a religious adage is relieved of having to deal with his basic emotional and interpersonal difficulties. In many cases there is a symbolic link between a person's compulsions and his underlying obsessions. In keeping with the obsessive-compulsive's dependence on the literal meanings of words, he symbolically does what his obsession suggests or demands. Thus, he literally cleanses himself of his feelings of personal filth and worthlessness by constant handwashing. By stomping on every crack in the sidewalk he is literally stamping out the inadequacies in himself, and by counting telephone poles or the slats in a fence he is trying to put everything in meticulous order, just as he is attempting to keep his inner feelings in numbered, tidy categories.

Each compulsive act or ritual in its early stages was both the product and the accompaniment of an obsession; however, after many weeks or months of compulsive activity the obsession often recedes to a large extent from the individual's field of awareness, and the compulsion seems to acquire an autonomy of its own. After years of compulsive rituals, a person may be unable to bring any of his original obsessions into his focus of awareness; he states that he persists hour after hour in his compulsive activity only because he feels an urgent need to do so and becomes anxious if he stops it.

Sullivan notes that there is a vast waste of time in a fully developed obsessive-compulsive disorder. The individual spends much of his life preoccupied with obsessive ruminations and carrying out compulsive acts. However, the alternative is intolerable emotional suffering. A good example of this is found in the frequent clinical picture of obsessive doubting and compulsive checking. The person obsessively doubts whether he turned off all the gas jets and water faucets in his home and he spends hours checking and rechecking them. In similar combinations of obsessive doubting and compulsiveness, the person's life is so filled with locking and relocking all doors and windows, filling out and rechecking each item on every sheet of paper that passes over his desk, and similar procedures, that he has no time either for the intrusion of his emotional pain or the actual work he is supposed to be doing.

In a severe compulsive neurosis, in which the patient spends 10 to 14 hours per day cleaning himself, the bathroom and every item he touches, interpersonal life comes to a complete halt, and it may remain paralyzed for months or years. At the cost of an incapacitating neurosis, interpersonal relationships, with all their threats of emotional pain, have been eliminated from the patient's life.

As noted above, Sullivan rejects the concept that obsessions and compulsions are devious expressions of hostility. In addition to the factors outlined earlier, he feels this idea has arisen erroneously because the person who tries to deal with an obsessive-compulsive becomes exasperated by his inability to break through the barriers of obsessive thoughts and compulsive acts and reach the patient. His exasperation leads him to feel that there must be a similar hostile basis in the patient.

THE THERAPY OF OBSESSIVE-COMPULSIVE DISORDERS

Sullivan had a particular interest in obsessive-compulsive patients and he lectured much about their difficulties and treatment. We shall sketch here only a few of his main principles in the psychotherapy of these patients. Much more material is found in the books containing selections from Sullivan's tape-recorded lectures and seminars, which are listed in the bibliography, and a general discussion of Sullivan's treatment methods is provided in our book on Sullivan's therapeutic techniques also listed there.

The obsessive-compulsive patient, especially if he has sophisticated knowledge about what is expected of him in psychotherapy, often fills each therapeutic hour with a pauseless flow of precise, staccato glibness. He may discuss his past and present experiences, his fantasies, his dreams and much else with what may seem to be hearty participation in therapy. An inexperienced therapist may for a long time feel that meaningful things are going on in treatment, when in fact the patient is simply using his skillfulness with words and word formulas to avoid the things that are really relevant to his problems.

The obsessive-compulsive patient carries into treatment the same techniques of massive miscommunication he employs in his day to day life. His flow of talk becomes especially rapid when something in therapy threatens to expose his true problems. Whenever therapy approaches his low self-esteem, his feelings of worthlessness, and his use of verbosity to avoid getting truly involved with people, he veers off into an urgent recital of some event in his life. The basic problem in treating obsessive-compulsives is that the fundamental tool of therapy, speech, is also the patient's major technique for avoiding recognition of his emotional and interpersonal difficulties. He throws up clouds of empty garrulousness to get therapy away from anything that is truly meaningful. At such times Sullivan, in his somewhat melodramatic way, would say, "Now we let the fog in."

Thus, obsessive-compulsive patients may go on for many months or years of psychotherapy with little benefit; if left to their own devices with a therapist who says little, they continue in this profitless way for indefinitely long periods of time. The psychiatric literature contains reports of obsessive-compulsive patients who had as much as 10 and 12 years of treatment with negligible results in such therapeutic situations.

Sullivan feels that as a rule it is desirable to isolate a particular current or past problem and, by searching comments and questions, to get the patient to examine carefully this well demarcated area. If this is not done, therapy often roams widely in emotionally flat and highly repetitive ways. In the early stages of treatment, the areas marked out for consideration frequently are aspects of current relationships in the patient's life. As treatment progresses, the specified topics tend to be in the patient's past life.

A meaningful formulation of some aspect of the patient's difficulties often mobilizes a certain amount of anxiousness in him. He feels stripped of the customary verbal devices he has long employed to avoid confrontation with some segment of his emotional problems, and he may become agitated or even panic-tinged. The therapist must exercise careful judgment in knowing just how far he can go without risk of making his patient worse or driving him from treatment. However, once the agitation subsides, the patient frequently can integrate this part of his new insight without discomfort. In many instances the therapist offers his interpretation in a tentative way, preceding it with phrases such as "Do you think it's possible that at times you . . ." and "Is it possible that what really happened was . . ." The patient often waves the interpretation aside or rejects it altogether, only to "discover" it himself at a later time when he can comfortably do so.

The basic issues which must in time be approached, as a rule repeatedly and from many angles in diverse interpersonal events and relationships, are 1) the patient's low self-esteem, 2) the interpersonal relationships which early in his life produced his feelings of worthlessness and 3) the ways he has employed words and word formulas to avoid awareness of these things. There sometimes is a certain amount of grieving as the patient sees all the lost interpersonal opportunities that his difficulties have caused him. Such insight, therefore, should come in fragments which are assimilated one by one.

Chapter 10

Other Neurotic Disturbances

THE SCOPE OF SULLIVAN'S WRITINGS AND LECTURES ON PSYCHIATRIC ILLNESS

The four neurotic disturbances about which Sullivan wrote and lectured extensively were anxiety and panic states, obsessive-compulsive disorders, hypochondriasis and hysteria.

As pointed out in the introductory comments to the second half of this book, Sullivan felt it was clinically valid to discuss only those disturbances which he had studied in an appreciable number of cases. He felt that 30 to 40 cases studied over periods of many months or longer constituted the minimum number of patients for formulating ideas about the nature and causes of any type of psychiatric difficulty.

He felt, therefore, that no psychiatrist or other mental health worker can collect during his professional career direct observations on enough patients to write definitively on the entire range of emotional illnesses. The most one investigator can do is outline basic principles of personality development, describe the techniques by which he gets his data and treats his patients, and discuss those psychiatric problems with which he has sufficient experience to form clear opinions. The rest must remain for those who come after him.

Having covered Sullivan's views on anxiety and panic states and obsessive-compulsive disorders in the two preceding chapters, we shall here consider his views on hypochondriasis and hysteria.

The Interpersonal and Emotional Functioning of a Person with Hypochondriasis

A person with hypochondriasis shifts his focus of awareness from interpersonal relationships to preoccupations with his physical state and possible dysfunctions in it. Instead of giving attention to what is occurring in his marital relationship, his associations with his children and his interactions with his work associates and others, he pinpoints his awareness on abdominal sensations, minor thoracic discomforts and other body sensations, and he ruminates on possible diseases that these things may indicate.

He nevertheless retains a strong need to communicate with people on some level. He does this by constant talk about his body sensations, his concern about diseases, the diagnostic tests he has had, the medications he is taking and related subjects. He discusses the physicians he has consulted and speaks at length about their opinions. Talk on this level becomes the main aspect of his personality which he presents to people, and it permits him to maintain interpersonal relationships and to interact with others. He is not truly seeking sympathy; his goal is broader and much more important to him. Though he obviously talks more to a sympathetic person than to a bored, rejecting one, he uses the same approach to everyone.

His hypochondriacal talk is thus an instrument for increasing his emotional security and for avoiding anxiety. It is a safe, nonthreatening area for interaction with people. It allows him to avoid awareness of any problems he may have with others, and any personality difficulties of his own which may be contributing to them. He does not talk and think about what goes on *interpersonally between himself and others;* he talks and thinks about what goes on *physically inside himself.*

Symptoms give significance to the person with hypochondriasis; without them he would feel interpersonally worthless and without a defined role. His medical concerns imply that he has value as a person, and they give him a socially acceptable set of activities that seem bustling to the casual observer, though they are found to be emotionally sterile and objectively baseless on profounder scrutiny. He consults physicians, has elaborate tests, undergoes brief hospitalizations for diagnostic purposes, buys medications and compares his symptoms with others who have true organic diseases. Like all emotional disorders, hypochondriasis can be mild or severe; it can vary from an occasional mode of conversation to an all-pervading way of life.

However, though hypochondriasis has certain problem solving qualities for the hypochondriacal person, it causes a host of secondary interpersonal difficulties. It contaminates his relationships at home, at work and in social circles. By virtue of his limited kinds of interactions, the hypochondriac is a less effective parent, a less satisfying marital partner and a less constructive coworker on the job. All his relationships are dampened and distorted by the hypochondriacal process. Still, it allows him to function within the limits it prescribes; without it he might develop far more crippling or ominous emotional and interpersonal problems.

The severity of a hypochondriacal process is determined by the degree of urgency the person has to exclude painful interpersonal issues from his range of awareness. When the hypochondriacal person can include a certain number of stressful events in his field of awareness his hypochondriacal preoccupations are less than when he must exclude almost everything of emotional consequence that transpires in his relationships with people. Also, the degree of a hypochondriacal difficulty in a person often varies from one epoch to another; when threatened by distressing interpersonal events, his hypochondriacal preoccupations worsen, and he may relate with people only on that level. When he is less menaced, his hypochondriacal ruminations tend to be less, and he can interact with greater feeling and in a broader range of activities.

The Interpersonal Causes of Hypochondriasis

Hypochondriasis tends to occur in a person with a pervasively depreciating concept of himself. This low self appraisal usually was produced by being reared in an interpersonal environment in which he was exposed to chronic deprecation as a person. Continual rejection, hostility and censure left him with the profound conviction that he was valueless. He frequently felt despair and hopelessness, especially if the feelings of worthlessness bred in early close relationships seemed to be confirmed by a series of interpersonal failures during the late juvenile period, adolescence and early adulthood.

By middle adolescence he doubts his ability ever to establish a truly satisfying, emotionally secure relationship with another person. At some time between late adolescence and early adulthood, he ceases to try to make contact with people in ways that involve emotional commitment. As a result he slowly loses his ability to evaluate others. The things that go on emotionally between people slip beyond his grasp, and he settles down to an interpersonal life based on preoccupations with his body and its possible dysfunctions; talk on these subjects become his safe, neutral ground for relating to people. In his desperate wishes to maintain contacts with others on some level, the hypochondriacal way of life becomes the sick solution to his emotional and interpersonal dilemma.

A further effect is a marked constriction of his capacity to perceive the feelings of others. He is thus protected from interpersonal pain in two ways—by talking only on the level of symptoms, body preoccupations and possible diseases, he gives out no information that may lead to interpersonal commitments and pain, and by constriction of his perceptions of the feelings of others, he receives no information which may distress him.

When something in his dealings with people becomes at all stressful, and emotional pain threatens to enter his field of awareness, his attention shifts quickly to body overconcern. As a result, people about him, in time, find their relationships with him sterile and baffling. Each time they try to involve him in a vibrant manner, they meet a flood of talk about symptoms, diseases and treatments, and the more urgently they try to contact him the more entrenched his hypochondriacal reaction becomes.

Finally, both the close people in his life and his lesser acquaintances desist from trying to form meaningful relations with him. They become indifferent or irritable, or simply seek their interpersonal satisfactions elsewhere, and the hypochondriacal person drifts into a narrow world populated with individuals who have no needs for dealing with him on a deeper level than his body overconcern.

Psychiatrists and other mental health professionals often see a hypochondriacal person only after he has been living in this barren interpersonal world for many years, and the optimal time for therapy has long since passed. The therapist finds he too can communicate with the patient only on the level of symptoms and ailments, and that if he attempts to push therapy beyond these limits, the patient flees the therapeutic relationship. It is beginning to threaten his long established pattern for remaining in the tolerable, though sick, emotional security. When patients are seen early in the course of a hypochondriacal development the chances for helping them are much greater. Psychiatrically alert family physicians, pediatricians and internists should identify hypochondriacal trends early and refer patients with such tendencies for aid from psychotherapists, child guidance clinics and other mental health services.

HYSTERIA

The Interpersonal Characteristics of Persons with Hysteria

In hysteria one or more symptoms, often beginning abruptly in a dramatic way, are interposed between a painful feeling, thought or interpersonal event and the individual's awareness of the disturbing precipitant. For example, a 23-year-old patient of ours suddenly developed hysterical paralysis of both her legs when her husband made sexual advances which she at that moment found repugnant; the paralysis allowed her to avoid sexual intercourse *without being aware of the true nature of her feelings.* The emotional problems of this patient were, of course, more complex than this simple incident indicates, but it demonstrates in almost a caricatured form the interpersonal mechanism of hysterical symptomatology.

A hysterical dysfunction occurs when an individual needs some kind of interpersonal and emotional satisfaction, but the satisfaction is threatening or repulsive to him. The dysfunction enables the person to avoid the menacing or distasteful activity. However, it does so at the cost of leaving the need unfulfilled, and of having an experience whose significance is beyond his scope of awareness. As we have seen in discussions of other types of disorders, the substitution of symptoms in place of awareness is treacherous. In such a process the individual does not acquire experience which could be assimilated and useful in meeting later problems with people. Also, the employment of symptoms as a way of solving interpersonal difficulties can become entrenched, and can spread into other areas of the person's life.

In the previous psychiatric syndromes, we have considered that the dysfunctions were interpersonal or emotional; they caused distortions in the person's ways of feeling and thinking or in his modes of interacting with people. In contrast, a hysterical dysfunction consists of a physical disability or a defect in sensory perception of gross memory; it is a paralysis, an anesthesia, a pain in some part of the body, loss of speech, blindness, or a blanket amnesia for a span of time. This is the main hallmark of a hysterical disorder.

In actual practice, a hysterical symptom usually has multiple interpersonal and emotional determinants. There is rarely the neat one-to-one relationship suggested by the simplified example sketched above. Moreover, a long course of personality development throughout childhood and adolescence produces the kind of person who is prone to develop hysterical difficulties when faced with conflict-laden interpersonal events.

Before proceeding to consider the childhood personality development of the individual who is predisposed to have hysterical symptomatology, we shall outline his emotional and interpersonal functioning as an adult. Sullivan's concepts of hysteria are more easily understood if approached in this order, and in his lectures and seminars he usually covers hysteria in this sequence.

The adult who is prone under interpersonal stress to develop hysterical symptoms has little true emotional investment in other people. He views them as objects who are either convenient or inconvenient to his needs of the moment, and he has little sensitivity to their needs and feelings. Other people are either audiences for his activities or things to be toyed with. In many cases he is not a difficult person so long as others do not collide with his wishes or object to the manner in which he wishes to live. However, when other people do interfere with his wishes or refuse to be nondemanding audiences, he may become dramatically angry, or tearful or sullen. He often finds a trivial excuse to flee a situation which is not conforming to his desires. When circumstances are not otherwise manageable he may develop hysterical symptoms.

He is, as a result of these personality qualities, apt to have interpersonal troubles, since most people are not content to serve him merely as objects or audiences for long periods of time. His life history therefore is often splattered with periodic interpersonal crises and recurrent bouts of hysterical symptomatology. His crises tend to be with his marital partner, children, parents, close work associates and others with whom he must have intense contacts. He usually functions better with the people with whom his activities are brief and superficial, for in such settings few demands are made on him and he has only minor obligations; moreover, he can depart from them quickly when they do not meet his egoistic interpersonal needs.

Hence, people who do not know a hysterical individual well may mistake him for being charming, well adjusted and able. The hysterical person often talks glibly about his relationships with others, and about love, duty and similar things with seeming sincerity. He can do this easily for he feels no real sense of commitment about any of the interpersonal and emotional ties he is discussing. A person who takes such talk at its face value frequently becomes perplexed and upset as he gets involved with a hysterical individual and finds that everything goes wrong in unexpected ways. Only in time does he grasp the inability of the hysterical person to relate to others on a truly profound level. Relationships with persons with hysterical personality problems are therefore treacherous, especially if the crises do not begin until after marriage and childbearing have taken place, or after firm vocational and social associations have been formed.

The Interpersonal Causes of Hysteria

The child who in later years will be predisposed to hysterical diffi-culties is both neglected and indulged throughout his formative years. He never has a truly warm relationship with anyone. Both his parents, and any other close persons engaged in rearing him, do not give him the tenderness and affectionate give-and-take that are crucial in sound personality development. The people who rear him go through the motions of infant and child care, but there are no strong feelings of any kind in the process. A casual onlooker may see nothing wrong with the way the child is being reared, but a sensitive observer soon discovers that there are no close bonds between the child and anyone. As a result, the child grows into a person who is incapable of making tender commitments in others. He also is unable to develop strong, meaningful feelings of any other kind in his dealings with people; they become what they will be all his life—either objects to be manip-ulated or convenient audiences for his activities.

At the same time the future hysterical person is indulged in a quite special way. One or both parents view him as a plaything. They do not see him as a growing personality, but as an ornament to the home, as a doll to be decorated, or as a bauble to be toyed with and admired. They play with the child, adorn him and admire him as they would an interesting inanimate object.

One or both parents are self-centered persons who see the child as an attractive embellishment of themselves. There is thus a tendency for parents with hysterical personality disorders to rear children with similar difficulties; they see the child as a cute, clever mirror of them-selves. They never grasp that the child is an independent, evolving person with his own character to form, his own suffering to go through and his own interpersonal problems to face and resolve. They give the child little, from an emotional point of view, and demand little from him.

This process goes on throughout childhood, the juvenile period and adolescence. Everything proceeds on a flat plane, devoid of deep emo-tional significance. The child never has an emotionally charged relationship with anyone, and he lacks the varieties and intensities of experience that produce a sensitive, discriminating individual who can participate intently with others. As a consequence, his life often is about as simple as he describes it, from an interpersonal point of view. When everything is going well he describes all his past and present relationships as "just fine," and he parrots all the conventional things that should be said about his upbringing and current activities. When in a crisis he describes everything as "terrible," and ascribes all problems to the shortcomings and malice of others.

During childhood and the early juvenile period the future hysterical person tends to solve the interpersonal difficulties he encounters at school and in other social situations by elaborate, dramatic daydreams. All children do this to a large extent, but the future hysteric does not give up his childlike, melodramatic daydreams as he grows older. Throughout adolescence and adulthood his daydream life remains grandiose and childlike. He does not have in his day-to-day life the kinds of meaningful experiences which allow him to evolve the more sophisticated, reality-linked daydreams that other people have. His emotionally barren life permits his daydreams to remain detached from everyday experience and to have a childish autonomy of their own.

He therefore arrives at adulthood with an extensive set of daydreams about himself, the people about him and the circumstances of his life which are more like those of a child than those of an adult. When he faces any kind of interpersonal difficulty or emotional turbulence he tends to use these childlike daydreams as the bases for his reactions, and he acts in florid, histrionic ways. He lacks the capacity for careful, reflective daydreams which prepare the way for mature action.

For these reasons, the hysteric's emotional responsiveness often has an extravagant coloring which is out of keeping with what is going on interpersonally at the moment. Separated from firm interpersonal governance and combined with an expansive, immature daydream life, his actions become exaggerated or irrelevant to his ongoing interpersonal situation.

When crises do occur, he is prone to go one step further and develop hysterical physical symptomatology. Just as every person is no more than an object to him and every group of people only an audience, his own body becomes an object whose functions are molded to meet his needs. He has acquired no other way of viewing all living things, including his own physical functioning. Its movements, sensations and capacities are, in ways outside his range of awareness, manipulated to solve the interpersonal dilemma in which he finds himself. His interpersonal problems are swept aside by hysterical major physical symptomatology or outright invalidism.

The particular kinds of physical symptoms which a hysterical person develops are determined by the concepts of body functioning which he had when his hysterical dynamism began in childhood. Thus, a hysterical paralysis of the hand or some other body organ follows a child's idea of what his hand or other body organ is, rather than the more sophisticated understanding of body structure which an adult has. A paralysis of the hand therefore stops abruptly at the wrist; it does not follow the more complex patterns which a physically caused dysfunction of the hand and arm would involve. In a similar manner, a hysterical seizure follows a child's concepts of the weird, impressive body contortions which constitute a "fit." The same general principle applies to the entire range of hysterical symptomatology.

Therapeutic Aspects of Hysteria

A central difficulty in psychotherapy with a hysterical patient is that he has never had meaningful relationships and dialogues with anyone. The therapist is therefore faced with the task of engaging the patient in a process he has not previously experienced, and which threatens him badly. In many cases the hysterical patient seems to talk well in treatment, but careful inspection of what he says, in time, reveals the same noninvolvement and superficiality he has in all other situations. He seems to be a "good" patient, but nothing of true significance is happening.

Another problem is that, as the patient talks, the therapist gradually realizes that many important things are left out of all his accounts of relationships and events in his life. Filling these gaps and bringing their contents at least partially into awareness is a major aspect of treatment. The patient has proceeded through life on such a shallow level emotionally that many events were beyond his grasp and understanding, or were dismissed as trivial. The relationships which are dismissed as "just fine" or "terrible" must be examined in depth, a thing the patient has never before done.

The patient's tendency to weave his elaborate, childlike daydreams into the fabric of his actual experiences creates many treacherous problems for the therapist. In time the therapist finds himself reflecting that many events the patient relates simply couldn't have happened that way, and that many of his ongoing relationships are probably far different from what the patient says about them. This is most likely to be so when the patient is talking with an urgency that may be convincing to an inexperienced therapist.

The therapist is presented in many cases with what Sullivan calls the patient's personal mythology. As actual events and immature daydreams are braided together in a flowing narrative, actual and fictional people are blended together to form the parents, marital partner, children, friends and other individuals the patient talks about. Real people are clothed with extravagant garbs and do extraordinary things. True incidents are colored by things that never happened, and untrue events are decorated with details from experiences the patient actually had. The hysterical patient's interpersonal life has been on so superficial a plane that truth and fiction do not have the decisive differences that they have for other people.

This points up a basic principle of Sullivan's interpersonal psychotherapy. Discussion of daydreams, or fantasies, is useful only to the extent that it leads the patient and the therapist to exploration of what actually did occur in the patient's life. Daydreams are valuable only as corridors that conduct the patient and the therapist to broader areas that contain the emotionally important relationships and events of the person's life. Extensive investigation of daydreams, or fantasies, is not a therapeutic end in itself. Treatment must deal with what actually happened, and is still going on, in the patient's interactions with people. His true life experiences, and not the romantic fictions of his personal mythology, constitute the material the patient and the therapist must deal with. This is particularly true of psychotherapy with hysterical patients.

Sullivan's concept of personal mythology has particular relevance to the psychotherapy of hysteria. An individual's personal mythology consists of combinations of memories, daydreams and interpretations of his relationships with people in his past and present life settings. Every person has a personal mythology. To some extent each individual colors the events of his life with his expectations and desires to make them more gratifying; in some cases, aspects of his personal mythology make segments of his life tolerable. However, most people have enough satisfying interpersonal experiences to permit their personal mythologies to remain reasonably close to what actually happened.

The person with a hysterical disorder has not had a large body of intense, emotionally meaningful experiences; his relationships have been superficial and have lacked vibrant gratifications that had strong impacts on him. His personal mythology is therefore only loosely attached to what really occurred in many areas of his life, and it can be modified in lavish ways to meet long-lasting needs or his needs of the moment. This is what he carries into psychotherapy and into his relationship with the therapist. Though his personal mythology reveals something about him, it operates as more of an obstacle than a help in the work the patient and the therapist must do if treatment is to solve his problems.

Our discussion in Chapter 7 of how Sullivan's principle of reciprocal emotions can influence the patient-therapist relationship applies with special force to the psychotherapy of hysterical patients. As we have seen, the hysterical person views people either as objects to be manipulated or as audiences for his dramatic, egoistic activities. His relationship with the therapist is therefore characterized by both these modes of interaction. The patient, in time, becomes adept at picking up clues from the therapist's comments, questions and silences about the kinds of material that the therapist wants to hear; he responds to the therapist's nonverbal reactions with material that seems to support whatever theoretical school of thought the therapist adheres to.

Thus, the therapist becomes the patient's audience and his object to manipulate, and the patient embroiders his personal mythology to make therapy as interesting as possible. In occasional cases, the patient even incorporates items from other people's lives and things he has read about psychiatry and psychotherapy.

Truly successful therapy of a hysterical patient requires alert awareness that these things can happen. If not, much mock therapy can go on for a long time. This process even extends into the results of treatment. It has long been known that, as far as a single hysterical symptom is concerned, most major hysterical dysfunctions such as a paralysis, an anesthesia or an aphonia, recede in time regardless of the type of therapy the patient receives. The therapist must be sufficiently honest with himself to ask if the recovery of his patient really supports the theories he employed or whether he has merely participated in one more superficial, fanciful event in the patient's life. He must ascertain if he has really reached his patient in a meaningful way and if the underlying hysterical modes of living have to some extent been changed.

Sullivan disapproves of hypnosis in the treatment of hysterical symptoms. Hypnosis is a *noninterpersonal* form of psychotherapy; there is no person-to-person interaction which is designed to increase the patient's awareness of the nature and causes of his difficulties. Moreover, as a result of the dramatic nature of the treatment, any improvement tends to be short-lived, and the patient becomes predisposed to other types of hysterical symptomatology.

Chapter 11

Schizophrenia

Sullivan spent the first eight years of his psychiatric career, from early 1922 to early 1930, working almost exclusively with hospitalized young male schizophrenics, first at St. Elizabeth's Hospital and then at the Sheppard and Enoch Pratt Hospital in the Washington-Baltimore area. Throughout his life he maintained a steady interest in schizophrenia and devoted more study to it than to any other psychiatric disorder. In the same sense that it is sometimes said that a comprehensive knowledge of Bach enables a musician to understand all other classical composers, Sullivan feels that a thorough knowledge of schizophrenia opens the way to understanding many aspects of both normal and abnormal interpersonal life.

He also feels that anything which, to a casual observer, seems unique in schizophrenia is merely something that occurs to a lesser extent in everyone else. All the phenomena of schizophrenia differ from normal emotional and interpersonal functioning only in degree.

Sullivan divides schizophrenia into two broad groups. The first, to which he usually is referring when he talks of schizophrenia, is a state of profound, disorganizing panic in which the patient has some loss of contact with reality. Paranoid coloring, special difficulties in feeling and relating to others, and a sense of impending disintegration of the personality are among the main features of this condition. In these acute schizophrenic panic states, the nature and causes of this disorder can be most clearly seen, and this is the optimum time for treatment.

145

The second group contains two conditions which occur secondarily in a certain number of persons with acute schizophrenic panic; these disorders have more serious prognoses and are more resistent to treatment. They are characterized by a wide variety of dysfunctions which develop as acute panic subsides and a persistent, incapacitating schizophrenic way of life evolves. He terms them the "paranoid transformation" and the "hebephrenic deterioration." By these terms, he means what most psychiatrists and other mental health professional workers today would call chronic paranoid schizophrenia and schizophrenic deterioration.

When Sullivan died in 1949, the phenothiazine medications and other antipsychotic drugs were not available. These medications, developed in the early and middle 1950s, have, of course, much improved the outlook for schizophrenia. They have moved the bulk of schizophrenic patients out of the second of Sullivan's two categories, with its poor prognosis, into the first category, which Sullivan considers schizophrenia in its essential form.

In our opinion, the development of antipsychotic medications has in no way invalidated Sullivan's views on schizophrenia. It has merely made large numbers of schizophrenics available for Sullivan's methods of study and treatment. These medications, moreover, have enabled psychiatric hospitals, community mental health centers, halfway houses, outpatient services and other facilities to function in a truly interpersonal manner in aiding these patients to achieve better ways of living.

THE INTERPERSONAL CAUSES OF SCHIZOPHRENIA— CHILDHOOD CONTRIBUTANTS

From infancy through adolescence the individual who, in time, will become schizophrenic never has a secure, comfortable relationship with another person. From the earliest phase of his life onward, he lacks the kinds of interpersonal associations that would enable him to evolve secure self-esteem and a sound self-system. He does not acquire capacities for anxiety-free living with people. In a deeply rooted way, of which he is at best dimly aware, he feels he is less than human and a failure as a person. All relationships with people, regardless of their surface appearance, seem potentially painful and menacing to him.

During infancy and early childhood, no close person treats the child with anxiety-free tenderness and affection. Cold, mechanistic attention or outright rejection characterize the attitudes of the persons who care for him. Frank hostility often is thinly camouflaged in each act of feeding, cleaning and dressing the child. In some cases the child is a shuttlecock in the parents' marital struggles, as each one blames the other for any problems or inconveniences the child causes, and for them he has little significance as a person.

Such emotional traumas rarely are evident to an uninvolved observer. They are hidden under façades of seemingly normal attention to the child; this makes his anxiety-laden experiences all the more devastating to him, for it is emotionally easier to deal with frank antagonism or rejection than to confront it garbed in apparently sound concern and attention.

As a result, the infant's initial concepts of the world and of himself are ominous. Using the terminology outlined in Chapter 1, the anxiety-producing (bad) nipple, the anxiety-producing (bad) mother, the anxiety-producing (bad) father and the anxiety-ridden (bad) me predominate over healthier perceptions of things, people and himself. A particularly foreboding development in the future schizophrenic is marked prominence of the panic-ridden (not) me in the child's emotional structure; this preponderance of the panic-ridden (not) me component in the individual's concept of himself is one of the basic features of the schizophrenic process.

The person thus emerges from his formative years with a continual expectation of pain and failure in every interpersonal relationship; his important contacts with people have led him to expect nothing else. He feels the presence of vague, intimidating forces in all aspects of the world around him, and he is troubled by a sense of eerie unsoundness within himself. This constant dread of threat in the world about him and in himself is what Sullivan calls the *malevolent transformation* of the future schizophrenic. Each interpersonal interchange and emotional reaction is tinged with menace.

As a rule, these developments are not manifested in the day-to-day activities of the child, adolescent or young adult who has suffered such interpersonal traumas. He retains strong needs for relationships with people. Despite the uneasiness within him and his apprehensiveness about closeness to people, he usually establishes workable adjustments with others for long stretches of time in the various areas of his life. Moreover, the childhood traumas of future schizophrenics vary much in degree from one person to another. In some individuals they are so overwhelming that a schizophrenic psychosis can be precipitated by mild interpersonal stress, whereas in others the interpersonal injuries of their formative years are much less intense, and severe conflicts with people are required to produce a schizophrenic break in adolescence or adulthood.

Although he feels that schizophrenia is the product of interpersonal traumas, Sullivan faces the possibility that in time physiological or genetic factors may be found which predispose some individuals to develop this order. His opinion, after surveying the research done in his own time on physical causes of schizophrenia, is that of the old Scottish jury verdict, "not proved." In our opinion, despite the vast amount of research done in the decades since Sullivan's death, the inconclusiveness of results and the lack of unanimity among investigators still sustain Sullivan's viewpoint. Sullivan adds that even if physical factors are in time found to incline some people to schizophrenia, they cannot explain the diverse phenomena of this condition. They can do no more than create the possibility of schizophrenia; the psychosis itself is the result of experience.

THE INTERPERSONAL CAUSES OF SCHIZOPHRENIA—
LATER CONTRIBUTANTS

A schizophrenic psychosis occurs when, in adolescence or adult life, damaging interpersonal situations cause the collapse of the emotional and interpersonal patterns of the individual's mature years, and he disintegrates into the kinds of feeling, thinking and interpersonal behavior which predominate in infancy and early childhood. That this viewpoint today seems commonplace is a tribute to the extent to which

Sullivan's ideas have quietly penetrated American psychiatry; when he proposed this concept in the 1920s it was novel. So pervasive, and yet so unrecognized is Sullivan's influence that Leston Havens of the Harvard Medical School has said that Sullivan "almost secretly" dominates American psychiatry. The reasons for this are traced in detail in our book *Harry Stack Sullivan: His Life and His Work;* to outline them here would require a long digression.

The type of interpersonal crisis which precipitates a schizophrenic illness is one that causes a collapse of self-esteem; the patient feels utterly worthless as a person, and not fully human. Some event, or series of events in his marital, familial, vocational, social and other areas have a disastrous impact on him; his concepts of himself and his interpersonal world disintegrate. All the emotional processes which have helped him feel emotionally secure and of some value cease to function, or function badly.

He is vaguely aware that an emotional and interpersonal calamity is happening to him, and this awareness unleashes panic. This panic is so severe and eerie that it is uncommunicable; neither during his acute schizophrenic break nor during his convalescence and beyond can the patient describe these feelings of personality disintegration and horror.

A feeling of his imminent dissolution as a human being floods the patient, and the world about him seems to be crumbling. His self-system, so carefully evolved over the years to make relationships with people comfortable, falls into disarray. As it decays, his capacities for relating to people become defective and atrophied. Communication with others becomes distorted, or virtually ceases. His capacity to concentrate the focus of his awareness on those things which are tolerable is lost, and many loathsome, uncanny, perplexing things dart in and out of his field of awareness in a helter-skelter manner. The term schizophrenia, drawn from Greek roots signifying a splitting of the personality, vaguely describes this fragmentation of control of awareness, with concomitant panic, as horror-filled impulses, feelings and thoughts overwhelm the individual.

A basic aspect of this process is full unleashing of the primitive panic-ridden (not) me experiences discussed in Chapter 1. Acute schizophrenia is the only psychiatric disorder in which the personality is so decomposed that panic-ridden (not) me infantile experiences flood the patient's field of awareness. When this happens all concepts of material objects, persons and oneself are overwhelmed.

Looking at this process from another viewpoint, the acute schizophrenic enters the prototaxic mode of experience described in Chapter 1. This is a timeless, spaceless world in which there are no sequences and in which cause and effect do not exist. Most important of all, it is a *noninterpersonal* world, since even the most elementary concepts of persons and oneself do not exist in it.

In talking of this, Sullivan states that schizophrenia is a withdrawal from interpersonal relationships by the channel of symbols. Symbols, mainly in the form of words and ideas, constitute the major means by which a person identifies both himself and the people around him. By words, ideas and other symbols, an individual establishes his own significance as a person. "Myself," "my mother," "my father" and innumerable other word-encapsulated symbols allow us to function as human beings. All these symbols disintegrate or become grossly deformed in an acute schizophrenic break, as a person withdraws from relationships with people.

Another central aspect of schizophrenia is the patient's loss of his capacity for consensual validation. He loses the ability to arrive at states of feeling, thinking and acting which are in harmony with the feelings, thoughts and actions of the people around him. Thus, he loses control of the ordinary meanings of ideas, perceptions, words, objects and people. As a result, all these things tend to acquire private meanings for him which he shares with no one else. For example, he often concocts new words, neologisms, which have special significances for him. Impairment of consensual validation destroys his capacity to retain a firm orientation on the opinions and intentions of others; delusions are one of the possible consequences. Defective consensual validation causes his gestures and body movements to lack their accepted social meanings; among the various results are schizophrenic mannerisms and stereotypies.

In general, the interpersonal events and relationships that unleash an acute schizophrenic break are those which assault a person's feelings of competence. An abrupt or long-lasting marital failure, or a vocational disaster, or emotional rejection by an important person or group of persons, or shortcomings as a parent or a host of other interpersonal conflicts or inadequacies can set a schizophrenic illness in motion. Sometimes these failures are dramatic and obvious even to the untrained eye; more often they are subtle, grinding difficulties which only careful investigation can elucidate. *These interpersonal failures in adolescence and adulthood tend to be similar to the failures he experienced in interpersonal living in infancy, childhood and the juvenile period.* He is subjected to depreciation as a person, rejection, hostility and treatment as a less than fully human person, just as he was during his painful formative years.

In addition, there may be a sudden upsurge of impulses within himself that he finds abhorrent. These upsurges, of course, occur in some kind of interpersonal situation that mobilizes them. Sullivan feels that in young male schizophrenics such feelings often are homosexual cravings, and that frightening conflicts over masculinity and feminity are significant in many of these patients.

All the processes discussed so far constitute only half the *clinical picture* a schizophrenic presents. At the same time that he is assaulted by panic and disintegration of his interpersonal environment he is struggling in desperate ways to find relief and to make some kind of adjustment, sick or healthy, to his dilemmas. He is attempting to make sense out of what is happening to him, and he is trying to construct new concepts of himself and his surroundings. These aspects of schizophrenia will be covered in various parts of the following three sections of this chapter.

COMMENTS ON THE VARIOUS TYPES OF SCHIZOPHRENIA

Like most interpersonally oriented psychiatrists, Sullivan feels that the various types into which schizophrenia is traditionally divided merely describe the particular symptoms which happen to be most prominent at any particular time. He accepts the use of such types, however, if it is clearly understood that they are merely verbal conveniences in talking about predominant processes in patients; they are not clear-cut categories of schizophrenia.

In his lectures and seminars he employs these diverse types as opportunities to consider the different kinds of emotional and interpersonal problems a schizophrenic patient may have.

Paranoid Type. A schizophrenic patient, ovewhelmed by panic and the dissolution of his interpersonal world, struggles to make sense out of what is happening to him and his surroundings. In doing so, he may concentrate on what seem to be sources of danger in his environment, and these vague feelings may crystallize into persecutory delusions.

The patient concludes, sometimes abruptly, that his suffering and perplexity are the results of malicious acts and attitudes of the people around him. He experiences a sense of relief as he feels he finally understands what is going on and identifies the people or malign forces who are attacking him and his environment. It is this sense of relief, combined with the feeling that his situation is now comprehensible, which make persecutory delusions so entrenched in many schizophrenic patients. This ominous solution to his problems decreases his emotional turmoil and gives him a course of action. He knows who his enemies are and can take precautions to defend himself against them. A wave of agitation may pass over him as he first establishes this paranoid solution, but the agitation wanes as he settles down to protecting himself against the people and forces who are harassing him.

Persecutory delusions serve another important function for the patient. They enable him to construct interpersonal links with people, sick as those links may be. These interpersonal ties are based on fear, hate, malice and the manifold machinations and plots which the patient feels are being mounted against him. However, the need for some kind of interpersonal relationships in each person is so strong that relationships on this basis seem better than none at all; the alternative is complete isolation in an interpersonal vacuum, and that is far more painful than the warped relationships created by persecutory feelings.

Persecutory delusions also raise the patient's self-esteem. He feels he must be an individual of some significance to be the object of so much plotting by so many. He feels blameless, ennobled and of increased value by innocently provoking such harassment. This sometimes leads to feelings of grandeur tinged with political, financial, religious or other delusions.

Catatonic Type. In a catatonic state the patient is so engulfed by terror, awe and uncanny dread that he sinks into withdrawn, mute immobility. He may not even attend to elementary nutritional and excretory functions; he must be spoon-fed, catheterized and shifted from side to side to prevent decubitus ulceration. Catatonia is the most extreme state of retreat from contacts with people and things.

However, most catatonics maintain some perceptiveness of what is happening around them, and a few of them are very alert behind the barrier of their silent immobility. In some cases, they abruptly lash out at seemingly threatening environments; they become briefly assaultive and destructive in states of catatonic agitation.

Hebephrenic Type. Sullivan, employing the terminology of the first quarter of this century, applied this term to patients who would now be classified as chronic, undifferentiated schizophrenics; it implied early onset and a grim prognosis. These patients were so badly traumatized interpersonally in their formative years that life with people is an unbearable experiment from which they retreat. They often are mute, absorbed in elaborate delusional worlds, and prone to body and facial movements which have undecipherable private meanings for them. The term hebephrenic has fallen into disuse in many psychiatric settings today, and readers of Sullivan's works are often misled by his employment of the phrases hebephrenic deterioration and hebephrenic dilapidation. Unfortunately, the editing of his published works lacks the footnotes which would be helpful to a contemporary reader.

Schizoaffective Type. This term was first introduced into the nomenclature in 1952, three years after Sullivan's death. Although he does not employ this term, Sullivan does deal with the exhilarated, overactive, forcedly jovial states that some schizophrenics enter into in their attempts to free themselves from feelings of worthlessness and dismal self-appraisal. He likewise considers the profound depressiveness which occurs in some schizophrenic patients as feelings of personal inadequacy flood them, with attendant possibilities of suicide.

Residual, Latent and Simple Types. The first two of these terms did not exist in psychiatric nomenclatures during Sullivan's lifetime; the third was prevalent, but Sullivan rarely employs it. Instead, he groups these patients among those who, in his words, achieve varying measures of "social recovery." By social recovery he means that the patient still exhibits evidences of the schizophrenic process but can adjust fairly well under some supervision by his family, or on the open sections of a psychiatric hospital or similar special setting. These persons have broad capacities for interpersonal activity, but their relationships are tinged with manifestations of schizophrenic feelings, thoughts and behavior.

INTERPERSONAL EXPLANATIONS OF VARIOUS KINDS OF SCHIZOPHRENIC SYMPTOMS

In this section we shall consider the interpersonal bases of many of the common phenomena of schizophrenia.

Hallucinations. As noted in Chapter 1, an infant in the early stages of his development cannot distinguish the differences between himself and the world about him. It is one vast blur in which discrete experiences tumble after each other without distinctions of sequence, time and space. The infant has no concepts, or only dim ones, of the differences between "I" and "you" and between "I" and "it."

As primitive modes of infantile experience invade the schizophrenic's field of awareness, he accordingly becomes confused about what are "I", "you" and "it." He is not sure whether the thoughts and feelings that course through his range of awareness originate within himself or outside himself. In time he feels that many of his thoughts and feelings emanate from outside himself, assuming the form of auditory hallucinations. These thoughts become audible voices which say menacing or reassuring things, depending on whether panic or reconstructive forces predominate at the moment. Auditory hallucinations are much more common than visual ones in schizophrenics since thoughts and feelings, by their shapeless nature, more easily take the form of voices than well-delineated visual objects.

Because of his impaired perception of the lines between himself and his environment, the schizophrenic also may be unable to determine whether tactile, gustatory and olfactory sensations are produced by things occurring in his surroundings or are the results of his own disordered state. These kinds of hallucinations usually are secondary to strong delusional forces, such as delusions that enemies are pumping poisonous gases into his room or that exalted religious acts are accompanied by fragrant incense and the perfumes of paradisiacal flowers.

The content of hallucinations is determined by the patient's interpersonal experience. If, during his formative years, he was subjected to continual censure and blame, his hallucinations tend to accuse him of crimes and repulsive deeds. If his sexual orientation is insecure, his hallucinations may accuse him of sexual perversions and lewd behavior. At other times hallucinations combat feelings of worthlessness and guiltiness with voices that assure him he is divinely protected and has a messianic, exalted mission to accomplish. A person never concocts hallucinations out of unexperienced interpersonal things; some facet of his life gives his hallucinations their content.

World Destruction and World Construction Concepts. In their attempts to establish logical meaning out of their feelings that the world about them is disintegrating in some weird manner, some schizophrenics develop world destruction concepts; they feel the world is coming to an end, or has already done so, or that their particular city or geographic locality is undergoing dissolution. Terrifying as such world destruction concepts are, they are less frightening than the idea that only the patient's world is disintegrating while everyone else's remains intact.

In reaction against the despondency that often accompanies world destruction feelings, a schizophrenic may go on to develop world construction fantasies. He feels that a new world is being built on the ruins of the old one, and in some cases he feels that in godlike or divinely inspired ways he is playing a major role in the construction of this new, better world.

Fragmentation of Thoughts. As outlined above, two of the central features of the schizophrenic's disorder are 1) his loss of control over his field of awareness, with repugnant thoughts and feelings racing through it in a chaotic way and 2) a shift to primitive, infantile modes of experience with their timeless, spaceless qualities and lack of senses of sequence and cause and effect. These factors explain the fragmentation of thought processes which is common in many schizophrenics. Words, phrases and ideas tumble forth in a disorganized manner. A person who has had much experience in working with schizophrenics may be able to piece together themes of preoccupation in the patient out of his jumbled thoughts, but the untrained observer rarely can grasp his threads of feeling and thinking.

Incomprehensibility of Speech. The factors outlined in the preceding paragraph account for much of the incomprehensibility of a schizophrenic's speech to an inexperienced observer. To these are added, in some cases, the nonverbal grunts and mumblings which are perhaps reminiscent of an infant's initial, inarticulate attempts to communicate. However, most of these inarticulate noises are attempts to convey the terrifying, chaotic contents of the panic-ridden (not) me segment of the personality which is prominent in acute schizophrenia. Since the not-me by its very nature is uncommunicable, the sounds the patient emits in trying to give some expression of the not-me transmit no meaning, even to an experienced mental health worker.

Blocking. Schizophrenic blocking occurs when a thought in progress is abruptly shunted out of the patient's field of awareness by uncommunicable things from the panic-ridden (not) me mode of experience. Awareness has shifted from the communicable to the noncommunicable. The patient often cannot find his original thread of thought after the panic-ridden (not) me eruption has receded from his range of awareness. This is but one more facet of the patient's loss of control over the content of his field of awareness as he flees from the threatening world of interpersonal relationships.

Neologisms. As noted above, neologisms are products of the schizophrenic's breakdown of consensual validation. As he loses meaningful contact with people, he constructs words which are interpersonally useless in communication; they have meaning for him, and no one else, but he employs them without awareness that they are noncommunicative. Neologisms are coined from fragments of the patient's experience. Emotionally charged, conflictual feelings frequently are bound up in neologisms, and a person skilled in treating schizophrenics may get insights into the patient's emotional turmoil by grasping their meaning.

Stereotypies. In a stereotypy some aspect of the patient's fragmented awareness becomes persistent and produces one or more repetitive physical actions. A stereotypy has some symbolic significance for the patient. Thus, a repeated lateral movement of the hand and arm may signify brushing aside repulsive thoughts and feelings, and stereotyped throat clearing and snorting may symbolize ejection of repugnant words and urges.

Mannerisms. A mannerism is composed of a set of exaggerated, elaborate physical activities that are either fragments of some prior experience, now reenacted out of its original context, or the accompaniment of a delusional role. For example, a backward tossing of the head and a steady stare may be a fragment of some experience in which the patient behaved in this way when in an alarmed or suspicious state, and a stiff, precise gait may be an accompaniment of delusions that he is a distinguished military personage. Mannerisms are interpersonally oriented poses and actions that are inconsistent with the person's ongoing interpersonal setting.

Mutism. Mutism may occur when the patient is flooded with the paralyzing terror of the panic-ridden (not) me mode of experience, and since this phase of experience is not communicable he sinks into speechlessness. On a more superficial level, mutism is yet another aspect of retirement from menacing interpersonal contacts.

Schizophrenic Stupor. Schizophrenic stupor occurs when the patient's various attempts, many of them sick ones, to comprehend what is happening to him have failed. Persecutory delusions, hallucinations, world destruction and construction fantasies, and all other processes have not helped him to reach some kind of accommodation to the turmoil within him. He therefore develops a rigid, immobile role, with apparent semicomatose detachment, to avoid further action and to defend himself from contacts with the malignant forces in his interpersonal surroundings. The stuporous schizophrenic sometimes constructs a universe within himself to replace the world he has lost, and remains raptly absorbed in it.

Hypochondriacal Symptoms During the Initial Phase of a Schizophrenic Illness. In a small percentage of cases, a patient goes through a hypochondriacal stage as he slips into a schizophrenic psychosis; this stage may last from a few days to a few months. A hypochondriacal process, as discussed in Chapter 10, moves a person's focus of awareness away from distressing interpersonal relationships to intense concern with the functions of his own body; he shifts his contacts with people to the nonthreatening level of talk about body sensations, symptoms and diseases. Hypochondriasis and schizophrenia share the common quality of flight from interpersonal activity to absorption in distorted ways with what is going on inside the person. In schizophrenia, however, the retreat is much more extensive and the deformation of interpersonal life is much more striking. Very few hypochondriacs become schizophrenics; their disturbances stop at the level of the hypochondriacal process.

Obsessive-Compulsive Symptoms During the Initial Phase of a Schizophrenic Illness. In the vast majority of cases, a person with an obsessive-compulsive disorder never develops a schizophrenic illness. The obsessive-compulsive disturbance enables the person to adjust to his emotional turmoil, though at the cost of the discomforts and inconveniences of his neurosis. However, in a small percentage of cases a person who is entering a schizophrenic psychosis passes through a phase of obsessive-compulsive symptomatology which may last from a few days to several months. He attempts to assuage the discomforts of his interpersonal life by encapsulating his distress in repetitive ideas, words, word formulas and physical acts, as outlined in Chapter 9. In the few cases in which this level of neurotic adjustment does not suffice to control the accumulating turbulence within him and the pain of his interpersonal stresses, a schizophrenic process may be unleashed.

A RECAPITULATION: SULLIVAN'S TRIPARTITE
VIEW OF SCHIZOPHRENIA

We are now in a position to present a comprehensive picture of Sullivan's view of the schizophrenic process. To this overall formulation he sometimes gives the name of *the tripartite view of schizophrenia.*

1) A schizophrenic illness is produced by a long series of painful past and ongoing interpersonal relationships and events. These traumatic relationships begin in infancy and continue during the childhood and juvenile years; their specific natures have been outlined earlier in this chapter. They leave the individual with marked feelings of worthlessness and inadequacy as a person, and feelings that all interactions with people are potentially painful and overwhelming. In adolescence or adulthood a particular interpersonal crisis, or accumulated stresses with people, make associations with others intolerable, and the schizophrenic disorder begins.

Consensual validation, the process by which a person maintains his feelings, thoughts and actions in realistic harmony with the people about him, crumbles. This is much the same as saying that, to a greater or lesser degree, the patient loses contact with reality. His concepts of the material world about him, the people in his surroundings and himself become distorted. Aware that some incomprehensible disaster is happening to him, or to the world about him, or both, panic deluges the patient.

A marked withdrawal from interpersonal relationships, which have become unbearably painful for him, begins, but this withdrawal is accompanied by perplexity, emotional distress and an urgent need to make sense of what the person is experiencing. Withdrawal from interpersonal relationships also involves impairment of the many security operations, forming in their totality the self-system, which have enabled the person to handle anxiety to a reasonable degree until this point in his life.

2) As he loses emotional and interpersonal contacts with people, the schizophrenic also loses control over the contents of his field of

awareness, and terrifying, loathsome, self-debasing feelings and thoughts besiege him. The panic-ridden (not) me mode of experience invades his focus of awareness, flooding him with eerie, uncanny, uncommunicable feelings.

In this process the patient becomes confused about what is "I," "you" and "it," paving the way for the subsequent development of various phenomena of schizophrenia.

3) In the third phase of Sullivan's tripartite view of schizophrenia the patient develops various feelings and ideas in an attempt to give coherence and meaning to the experience he is going through.

This produces a new state which is a synthesis of speculations and ideas that constitute, when not influenced by successful therapy, a new way of looking at himself and the world about him. When it is persistent, Sullivan sometimes terms it the schizophrenic way of life. The patient, for example, may develop world destruction concepts to explain the drastic changes that seem to be occurring in his environment, and world construction concepts to build a new world in which he can find a tolerable, or even elevated role. He evolves persecutory delusions to explain the malice which he senses in people around him and grandiose delusions to defend himself against feelings of insignificance and inadequacy. Auditory hallucinations, and occasionally other types of hallucinations, give palpable forms to the threatening or exalting feelings and thoughts that overwhelm him; his impaired ability to establish the boundaries between himself and his surroundings facilitate this process. In the various other ways outlined in the two preceding sections, he constructs a new mode of experience to give his existence meaning and to make sense out of what seems to be happening to him and his environment.

The first two stages of this tripartite process produce acute schizophrenic panic states, and the third stage produces the more advanced schizophrenic clinical pictures.

The length of time a schizophrenic patient spends in these individual phases varies a lot. The first two stages may be traversed in a matter of hours, or they may continue for several months. The third stage may last from a few days to many years. The lengths and intensities of these stages are, of course, greatly influenced by whether the patient receives prompt, appropriate treatment. Their durations and outcomes are, of course, much affected by the severity of the patient's past and ongoing interpersonal traumas.

THE THERAPY AND OUTCOME OF SCHIZOPHRENIC DISORDERS

Sullivan taught and wrote a great deal about the treatment of schizophrenia. In a book of this nature we can do no more than sketch a few of his viewpoints. More detailed information about his therapeutic techniques in general and regarding schizophrenia in particular may be found in his works listed in the bibliography of this book, and the final chapter of our book *The Treatment Techniques of Harry Sullivan* is a guide to that body of material.

As indicated earlier in this chapter, the development of the antipsychotic medications since Sullivan's death does not invalidate his concepts of schizophrenia and the interpersonal aspects of its treatment. Pills do not change the past life experience of a person, nor do they resolve ongoing interpersonal traumas. However, the antipsychotic medications have proven invaluable in decreasing the inner turmoil in the vast majority of schizophrenics, thus making them amenable to interpersonal measures. These interpersonal measures help them to return to their prepsychotic levels of adjustment, and often to go on from there to achieve degrees of emotional and interpersonal health they previously lacked.

Interpersonal treatment techniques include healthy experiences in specially organized psychiatric hospitals, new experiments in living in halfway houses and similar settings, and exploration of current and past interpersonal warps in group psychotherapy and individual psychotherapy. They also embrace direct treatment of the patient's closest interpersonal situations, as in family therapy, counseling of the patient's relatives to create a healthier environment for him, and kindred measures.

The two therapeutic measures Sullivan explored in his work with schizophrenics were 1) individual psychotherapy and 2) the organization of psychiatric wards designed to give the patients new experiences in healthy living. Though many workers in previous times had advocated the humanitarian organization of psychiatric wards, Sullivan was the first person to reason that, if unhealthy interpersonal living made people sick, healthy interpersonal experiences ought to aid them to recover. He was the first person to set up carefully planned interactions on a psychiatric ward to help patients in ways *specifically* designed to meet their individual needs and the needs of the patient group as a whole.

These two treatment approaches are more interlocked than might at first seem evident, for in organizing a therapeutic environment, the principles of individual psychotherapy are to a large extent merely extended and modified to suit the group situation.

We shall first survey briefly Sullivan's views on individual psychotherapy of schizophrenics, and shall then outline his concepts of a therapeutic experience on a ward in which patient-staff interactions and patient-patient interactions are designed to make interpersonal living less menacing to patients and thus facilitate their recovery.

In an acute panic state in the initial phase of a schizophrenic illness, the patient has little ability to communicate with the therapist. His field of awareness is so disturbed by the terrifying, uncommunicable contents of his panic-ridden (not) me phase of experience, and he finds relationships with people so threatening, that he is unable to express his feelings and thoughts in any kind of dialogue, verbal or nonverbal. Outgoing information from him virtually stops. The therapist, of course, from his knowledge of the schizophrenic process, has a general understanding of what the patient is experiencing, but his understanding is based on the patient's total clinical picture rather than any specific thing the patient says or does.

However, despite his turbulence and perplexity there are far fewer impediments than would be expected in the patient's absorption of communication from the people in his environment. In his distractible terror, the schizophrenic person is much more alert to the feelings, attitudes and words of those around him than a casual observer might guess.

Communication from the therapist at this point should be limited, and his nonverbal behavior is probably as important as what he says. Communication is never pushed or insisted on; it is, so to speak, put at the disposal of the patient, and patient can assimilate it to the extent that it is comfortable for him to do so. The therapist should get across to the patient that he is sincerely interested in him as a suffering person, and is taking pains with him. He should convey the impression that he has at least a limited conception of what the patient is experiencing. Above all, the therapist must not be patronizing or blandly reassuring; he should transmit a feeling of deep concern and an earnest desire to understand and help.

Some therapists can do this and some cannot, and it can be taught to therapists only to a certain extent. Instruction can give people knowledge more easily than it can give them sensitivity to the pain of others. Schizophrenic patients have an almost uncanny ability to grasp quickly who are the phonies and who are the truly interested people; they know which therapists consider them as cases and which ones consider them as persons.

The therapist must not impart impressions of frustration, impatience or discouragement; he should leave if such feelings begin to arise in him. The patient does not want to frustrate the therapist; he simply feels it is unsafe at this point, and perhaps for some time into the future, to attempt to form any kind of relationship.

As his initial terror subsides, or while it still afflicts him to some extent, the schizophrenic has pressing needs to make some kind of sense out of the experience he is passing through. He does not require extensive comprehension of it; indeed, anything more than the most superficial understanding is beyond him, and would alarm him if offered. He needs the feeling that even if he has no comprehension of his situation, somebody else does and that person will in time aid him to understand it. Hence, at this stage one of the therapist's most important tasks is to get across to the patient that, no matter how chaotic his experiences have been, the therapist has reasonably clear ideas about what is going on, and will help the patient to grasp these ideas and to emerge from his distress and confusion.

In the early phases of treatment the therapist in many cases says little, but what he says should get the above outlined messages across simply and forcefully. He then stops. He may sit in silence with the patient for a while, and by his nonverbal behavior he indicates a willingness to be of use. A slight encouraging smile of earnest interest, a brief pressure on the patient's hand to indicate a contact that is offered but not pushed, and a quiet, unhurried entrance and exit from the patient's room or the hospital's day room, are often as important as the therapist's words. Sullivan states that the therapist at such times can usually say whatever is advisable in half a dozen sentences, or so. The patient is very cautious about interpersonal contacts, and more active therapy is more apt to harm than help him.

As the patient's panic recedes, or in intervals of more calmness and communicability, the therapist may talk in nonpenetrating ways, and in circumspect amounts, about the kinds of interpersonal turmoil that apparently have caused the patient's illness; he may suggest that things in the patient's past have been agitated by recent or ongoing events. Complex inquiries and explanations are avoided.

Sullivan feels that many communicable schizophrenics tend to agree with any formulation of their trouble that appears to explain it, or at least indicates that the therapist feels he understands it. Hence, Sullivan states that an unwary or doctrine-dedicated professional person can get the impression from a convalescent schizophrenic that the patient's positive responses and subsequent improvement support whatever theories he has about the patient's illness, regardless of whether they are indeed germane to the patient's true interpersonal dilemmas.

The optimum time to begin treatment of a schizophrenic is during the initial state of panic and perplexity. If months or years elapse before interpersonal treatment begins, the prognosis is much less favorable. This is, of course, a common psychiatric observation, but Sullivan's views on schizophrenia explain it in a manner that removes it from the realm of flat descriptive psychiatry. He formulated these opinions during his most intensive work with schizophrenics in the 1920s, and lectured widely on them. The specificity of his measures, and his detailed reasons for them, were unprecedented. Many later writers have taken over his viewpoints, weaving them into the fabric of

American psychiatry, often without citing their debt to Sullivan in these and other respects.

After a schizophrenic has emerged from his stage of panic and personality disorganization, an experienced therapist may start to explore the interpersonal events that provoked his psychosis. Investigation of the past interpersonal traumas that predisposed him to his illness depends on the patient's ability to tolerate such work without undue anxiety and the threat of a relapse. Blunt probing is at all times avoided. The patient, to a large extent, sets the pace and depth of treatment.

Many schizophrenics, even when well on the road to recovery, feel that, if other people are interested in them, their intentions are exploitive and their good will is feigned. Caution is therefore imperative throughout treatment; the therapist's antennae are always tuned to catch the first signs of suspicion and alarm. In many cases, a schizophrenic feels that, when another person discovers how worthless and loathsome he is, he will abandon him in disgust. When paranoid coloring is present, the patient is at most times scanning the therapist to discover evidence of self-interest under the guise of apparent helpfulness. A major facet of the therapeutic task, therefore, is to gain the trust and confidence of the patient. The schizophrenic has never had a truly comfortable, nonexploitive relationship, and he suspects that this new relationship will be no exception to the rule.

Looking at all these things from a somewhat different point of view, the therapist is employing his own personality as a tool to help a person who has little trust in the possibility that associations with people can actually be comfortable and beneficial to him. To get this job done, while still retaining his role as a professional person, is a central feature of interpersonal psychotherapy. Treatment must never deteriorate into a solicitous friendship. Sullivan states repeatedly that the emphasis must always be on the *work* (Sullivan's word) which the patient and the therapist are doing in their joint venture.

Schizophrenic withdrawal from human contacts is never total, regardless of how long the illness lasts. Even long neglected, chronic, "back ward" patients retain residual capacities for interaction with people. The therapeutic techniques outlined here apply to all schizophrenic patients, but expectations of improvement must be curbed when treatment is tardy and the disorder has been long entrenched.

As a schizophrenic becomes more accessible, one of the main tasks is to provide him with an environment in which interpersonal relationships are encouraging; he is in diverse ways led back across the interpersonal gap between psychotic withdrawal and comfortable life with people.

Sullivan feels that a psychiatric ward which is elaborately designed to meet each patient's needs is an invaluable instrument to accomplish this. In 1929, he set up, at the Sheppard and Enoch Pratt Hospital on the outskirts of Baltimore, the ward which was the forerunner of all the therapeutic communities, milieu therapy settings and similar organizations that have been evolved since then. He was the first therapist to give extensive psychotherapeutic training to hospital aids, some of whom had no more than a grade school education, and he held long, daily conferences with all his ward personnel to discuss how they should interact with patients to encourage their recovery.

Sullivan was willing on this ward to experiment with any kind of interpersonal device which might be useful. For example, thinking that conflicts over homosexual urges might be factors in some patients' emotional tumult, he had some of his aides discuss their adolescent experiences with mutual homosexual masturbation within the hearing of the particular patients who perhaps were struggling with insecure sexual orientations. Patient by patient, he discussed with the aids and other ward personnel the apparent problems of each schizophrenic, and outlined measures for dealing with them. He held individual psychotherapeutic sessions with each patient, sometimes with an aide present to give it a group interpersonal atmosphere. He apparently was the first therapist to have a stenographer present to take down verbatim everything that was said, so it could be examined afterward in planning further experiences for the patient on the ward; wax cylinder recorders and tape recorders for clinical use had not then been developed. Such measures, crude as they were, had never been employed previously on a pyschiatric ward.

Sullivan lectured and wrote extensively about this ward, but never in book form, and it made him one of the most discussed psychiatrists of his day. He demonstrated that the results of such treatment were better than those of patients who did not have it; both the percentages of complete recoveries and social recoveries (improved patients who still had evidences of their disorders) were superior to those obtained by other treatments then utilized.

Using this ward, Sullivan put into concrete form his concept of schizophrenia as an interpersonal disorder, treatable by interpersonal methods. A review of the innumerable variations and refinements of his methodology which are now standard features of American psychiatry, and their slow spread to other parts of the world, would involve us in an unnecessary dissertation.

Sullivan recognizes that a small number of persons are so traumatized in their formative years that they sink into chronically incapacitated states despite the most energetic and ingenious treatment. Life in some kind of supervisory setting is necessary. These are the people who have found interpersonal ventures so uniformly disastrous that they have given up any hope of living in contact with people. They are so completely demoralized and suffer such profound despair that they see no possibility of success as human beings. Fortunately, the number of schizophrenics who eventually fall in this category is far smaller than when Sullivan began his work on this disorder in the 1920s.

Sullivan feels, finally, that everything that can be done to make society interpersonally healthier is relevant to the prevention of its most common emotional disaster, schizophrenia. Though he formed this viewpoint during his first few years in full-time psychiatric work, he did not begin systematic investigation of this facet of schizophrenia until his last disease-ridden years.

Chapter 12

Other Psychotic Disorders

SULLIVAN'S COVERAGE OF PSYCHOTIC DISORDERS

The only other psychotic conditions about which Sullivan lectured and wrote extensively were the paranoid states. Although he occasionally lectured on manic disorders, depressive conditions and organic brain psychoses, he invariably prefaced such discussions by saying that he had not sufficient experience in treating patients with these disorders to say anything more than could be found in conventional psychiatric books. He talked about them only to round out courses of instruction which his position required him to give from time to time. As noted at the beginning of the second half of this book and in the early paragraphs of Chapter 10, such restraint in distinguished psychiatric pioneers is uncommon. Sullivan never went further in developing his interpersonal approach to psychiatric illnesses than his clinical experience allowed him.

The paranoid states are traditionally defined as conditions in which patients have persecutory feelings without signs of a concomitant schizophrenic process. Many terms are used to separate the various syndromes, or disorders, grouped under the broad heading of paranoid states. They include paranoid personality disorder, paranoid state, paraphrenia, paranoia and others. Different nomenclatures categorize them in slightly different ways. A paranoid condition may be so mild that it merely consists of a suspicious coloring, and is usually termed a paranoid personality disorder, or so severe that complicated delusional feelings and ideas penetrate almost every aspect of the patient's life, as in paranoia.

Like Sullivan, we shall not attempt to subdivide and pigeonhole these conditions; we shall consider them all under the simple heading of paranoid states. We shall occasionally employ the traditional terms, such as paranoia and paraphrenia, only to orient the reader who has long been accustomed to such terminology.

THE INTERPERSONAL CHARACTERISTICS
OF PARANOID STATES

A person with a paranoid state feels that one or more other individuals have malicious intentions toward him. The nature of the disorder in any particular patient depends on how frequently persecutory feelings occupy his field of awareness and how much emotional upset they arouse in him. In a paranoid personality disorder, suspicious feelings may be absent from the patient's focus of awareness for long periods of time, and they cause relatively little turmoil in him. In paranoia, persecutory delusions are almost constantly present in the patient's range of awareness and cause him much distress. Secondarily, the person's persecutory feelings have widely different impacts on his interpersonal life; in a paranoid personality disorder the individual's associations with people are influenced much less than those of a person with paranoia.

Sullivan feels that there are various ways in which a person may develop a paranoid state. In this section we shall outline two of them.

In the first of these the paranoid state is a residual of a schizophrenic illness. In the second it is the result of the process of *malevolent transformation* described in Chapter 10.

In some cases, a paranoid state is the residue of a transitory schizophrenic illness. The acute schizophrenic panic may last from a few hours to several days, during which time menacing forces of his panic-ridden (not) me surge through his focus of awareness. As this state subsides, small residues of his panic-ridden (not) me mode of experience become invested in persons around him. They thus acquire a vague threatening and malicious tinge for him. His panic-ridden (not) me mode of experience recedes in all respects but one; it continues to color faintly his view of one or more persons. Such coloring varies greatly in degree from one patient to another, and determines the kind of paranoid state he develops.

Many of these persons never again suffer an illness which can properly be called schizophrenic, since they lack all the other features of schizophrenia. They may function fairly well in their vocational and social lives, but there always is a suspicious aloofness which no one penetrates. These things taint their relationships with their marital partners, children and other close persons. The people they mingle with socially may notice nothing more than a certain unwillingness to become closely involved with anyone. Many of these individuals in time become adept at hiding their suspiciousness behind a façade of apparent ease and camaraderie, and only occasionally do their paranoid feelings glint forth.

In other cases, a paranoid state is the result of the slow elaboration of the *malevolent transformation* outlined in Chapter 10. During infancy, childhood and the juvenile period, the growing person experiences much rejection, irritability and depreciation from the close people around him. His life experiences are contaminated with the feelings of hostility in the individuals around him and, in response to external hostility, within himself. These vague but strong feelings in time take specific forms, and the person develops convictions that several or more people about him have sinister intentions toward him. He feels he must remain constantly on guard to protect himself against exploitation and ill will.

In addition, feelings of inadequacy and inferiority linger on the fringes of his field of awareness. It is as if he were, in essence, saying to himself, "I am of little value, and hence people despise and dislike me. I can never be comfortable with them; I must be on guard that they do not exploit me because of my weakness."

In severely paranoid individuals a compensatory process sometimes is added; feelings of exaggerated self-importance develop. The patient feels, in a sense, "I am not, in fact, inferior and worthless. My difficulties are caused by the malicious attitudes and harassments of those who envy my superior qualities. However, I see through it all and shall foil them." Such feelings of superiority, which at times verge on delusions of grandeur, become an imbued feature of the paranoid state, giving the patient a more comfortable, though obviously sicker, adjustment.

In some persons with long-standing paranoid states the persecutory elements at times subside for varying stretches of time. During these periods the patient's focus of awareness may shift from the malicious things which he feels are going on *around* him to possible sinister things happening *inside* him. This produces a period of body overconcern which may assume the proportions of hypochondriasis. Such hypochondriacal states may last from a few weeks to several months or more. In almost all cases the hypochondriacal process ceases in time, or at least decreases in intensity, and the paranoid state once more dominates the clinical picture.

THE INTERACTIONAL CAUSES OF PARANOID STATES

Sullivan, for teaching purposes, divides the development of many paranoid illnesses into five stages. Recognizing both the clinical artificiality and the didactic usefulness of such a scheme, we shall follow his outline.

There is some overlapping among these five stages and the two processes of paranoid development outlined in the preceding section. Sullivan recognizes that the complexities of psychiatric disorders often defy neat, exclusive pigeonholing, and occasional overlapping is the inevitable consequence.

1) The person with a paranoid state has a prevailingly negative view of himself. During his formative years he did not experience sufficient affection, acceptance and approval to give him the feeling that he is a worthwhile person. Instead, he experienced much hostility, depreciation and rejection. He cannot ascertain who is to blame for his situation; he cannot grasp that the people about him are to blame because of their persistent, debasing attitudes toward him. The idea that the basic warp is in them, and not in himself, never occurs to him.

2) The individual's low appraisal of himself prevents him from seeking the kinds of interpersonal relationships and activities which could correct, at least partially, the earlier damage. At school, in the neighborhood and in social groups his feelings of inadequacy prevent him from forming the close relationships which might improve his unhealthy view of himself; expecting only further interpersonal pain, he avoids the contacts which could help him.

With a courage and self honesty that is not always found in distinguished psychiatric pioneers, Sullivan often asks the questions that could undermine his own viewpoints. At this juncture, for instance, he poses the following questions: Why doesn't the future paranoid child, or the adult with a paranoid state, sort people out in terms of his emotional needs? Why doesn't he separate out some persons who would treat him with the supportive relationships that would give him corrective interpersonal experiences and gradually seek closeness with them, and shun associations with those who might by their irritability and rejection aggravate his problems? Why, by such interpersonal measures, can't he solve his paranoid difficulties?

The answer seems to be that during infancy, childhood, the juvenile period and early adolescence, the same people give a person both his physical security and emotional rejection. The parent who is hostile and depreciating toward the growing paranoid child also provides him with food, clothing and innumerable other things that are necessary for his physical welfare. The damaging people both traumatize and protect the child; they are both malicious and helpful. This fact robs the future paranoid person of the capacity to distinguish between those who will harm him and those who will help him emotionally as his interpersonal life slowly expands outside the home in the juvenile period and adolescence. Such a discrimination would require a fineness of judgement and a level of understanding of interpersonal relationships which almost no children and paranoid adults have. Hence, all people seem uniformly dangerous to him, and separation of those who would help and those who might harm him emotionally would require a body of experience he never had.

For this reason, simultaneous physical brutality and emotional rejection often cause less long-term trouble to a child, though his short-term suffering may be severe. If the parent who rejects him emotionally also malnourishes and beats him, the child does not struggle with the confusion which the future paranoid child faces. This is no argument, of course, for mistreating children physically, but it throws light on another aspect of Sullivan's searching questions.

3) In the many interpersonal events of adolescence and early adulthood there are further accretions to the paranoid process. Occasionally someone may go out of his way to try to establish a close bond with the patient, and this is more likely to frighten than reassure him. If such attempts are vigorously pushed they may augment the patient's paranoid trends. The patient's feelings and thoughts may, in essence, be: "He wants to form a close relationships with me so he can afterward reject me and cause me pain." Forced close associations, as in academic groups, military service groups, work teams and similar groups may actually exacerbate the patient's persecutory feelings.

Despite the pain and repeated interpersonal failures produced by a paranoid condition, it serves a limited cohesive function. In his warped way the person has vibrant associations with people. He is constantly watching them, moving to outwit their maneuvers against him and preparing to foil their future moves. Sick as these interpersonal struggles are, they are more bearable for a paranoid person than no interactions at all. Interpersonal isolation would be intolerable, and in the absence of any contacts with people, his paranoid feelings would proliferate in ominous ways.

In some cases a paranoid state begins, at least so far as its clinical manifestations are concerned, in an abrupt manner. The basic personality traumas and lingering perplexity have long been present, and at some point the patient feels that he suddenly "sees it all." He feels that in a moment of rapid insight he rips the masks off the people about him and sees their malignity fully for the first time. Innumerable confused experiences, past and present, now seem clear to him. Such rapid eruptions of full-fledged paranoid states usually occur in late adolescence or the early stages of adulthood.

4) In still other cases a paranoid state evolves quickly in a person predisposed to it by traumatic past experiences through a process which Sullivan terms "a massive transfer of blame." Everything that

is defective in a person's past and ongoing life is attributed to the ill will or machinations of one or more other individuals; a vast relief is suddenly experienced as the person finds a paranoid solution for his emotional turmoil and interpersonal misadventures. By massively transferring blame to others he "sees through" it all and frees himself from responsibility for many failures.

This is obviously a variant of the process outlined above in section three, but it has some special interpersonal features. This is particularly likely to occur when a person, already somewhat prone to paranoid feelings, has, for many years, lived in an environment in which massive shifts of blame were frequently used to bolster self-esteem. Thus, in a family the blame for everything that goes wrong may be put on one or more children, and in a marriage one or both marital partners may rescue his self-esteem by a massive transfer of blame to his spouse. The same may occur in social and vocational organizations, in which all disasters are shrugged off by massively blaming some allegedly malicious group that has caused all the trouble. Whatever the case, years of living in a small or large group in which massive transfers of blame have been habitually employed to gain emotional relief may contribute to the abrupt onset of a paranoid state in a person whose early life experiences have predisposed him to such a disorder.

5) Since some paranoid states are notoriously resistant to treatment, a few of their long-term interpersonal consequences should be pointed out.

When a paranoid state has been present for many months or a few years, the patient in some cases develops a complex body of grandiose daydreams to fill the interpersonal gaps in his life. This may actually contribute to better adjustments in his relationships with others, so long as his associations with them remain on a superficial plane and true closeness never develops. By elaborate speculations and daydreams, the patient feels he has successfully held his potential persecutors at bay so he can form what seem to be socially acceptable relationships with them. The patient's guard is always up, but he feels confident in his abilities to outwit them whenever necessary.

Such a paranoid person tends to have certain characteristics in his interpersonal behavior which the trained eye can sometimes detect. He is intently observant of others and sometimes has a remarkable memory for everything his companions say and do. He frequently looks at them with a subtle smile, a slight narrowing of the eyes and a gentle backward tilt of the head; his whole bearing says, "I see what you're up to, but I'm one step ahead of you." Sullivan advises therapists always to be alert to the vast amount of information which paranoid persons, and all others, are constantly transmitting in their nonverbal behavior.

Depression, occasionally so severe that it involves suicidal thoughts, sometimes occurs in a person with a long-term paranoid state. The emotional barrenness of his life, combined with his underlying feelings of worthlessness and hopelessness, precipitate depressive feelings. The depression often can be successfully treated, even when the paranoid state remains unchanged.

The person with a paranoid state in many cases does not develop the capacity to have a comfortable relationship with a person of the opposite sex. This is caused by his continual suspiciousness about the motives of others, his constant vigilance against an involvement in which he could be exploited, the subtle depressiveness to which he occasionally is subject, his underlying feelings of worthlessness and his inability to form a long-term, close relationship that is free of paranoid speculations. Sullivan feels that it is this failure to be at ease in full heterosexual development that has led to erroneous views that paranoid disorders are in some way caused by homosexual impulses. He feels that homosexual feelings, either aware or unaware, have nothing to do with the development of any kind of paranoid disorder.

A few persons with paranoid states can establish interpersonal relationships which resemble closeness with people who are manifestly their social, economic and cultural inferiors. These persons, by virtue of their clear inferiority, do not threaten the paranoid person; they do not have enough power, talents and prestige to carry out malicious designs against him. A kind of apparent closeness, thus, may develop in such a situation, and to some extent, many of the paranoid persons's interpersonal needs may be met in this manner.

Chapter 13

Some General Observations on Diverse Psychiatric Disorders

We have finished our coverage of those psychiatric disorders about which Sullivan lectured and wrote extensively. He left for succeeding generations the task of investigating the interpersonal causes and treatment of the remaining kinds of psychiatric difficulties. However, he made some interesting comments on various types of psychiatric dysfunctions and he discussed a few related topics. In this chapter we shall cover these subjects.

THE ONE-GENUS POSTULATE

A central feature of Sullivan's approach to psychiatric disorders is the one-genus postulate. This states, in Sullivan's somewhat cryptic terminology, that *everyone is much more simply human than otherwise.* Though he formulated this principle in 1938, he did not emphasize it in his teachings until the last few years of his life.

Sullivan includes various things in his one-genus postulate.

Firstly, he stresses that everything we see in those persons whom we call psychiatrically ill is present to some extent in those individuals whom we consider psychologically healthy. The differences are of degree rather than nature. For example, the differences between a shy individual, a person with a schizoid personality disorder and a schizophrenic are merely ones of degree; they are all, in varying dimensions,

176

uncomfortable in close relationships with people and tend to withdraw from them. Nothing—emotional, interpersonal, biochemical or biophysical—occurs in psychiatric illness which is not seen in healthy people to some extent.

The implications of this are far-reaching. It indicates that the emotionally healthy and the emotionally sick have merely had somewhat different experiences in their relationships with people. This principle also stresses that the places at which we draw lines between normality and abnormality are always somewhat arbitrary, and vary from time to time and from one culture to the next. This postulate robs psychiatric difficulties of any suggestion of bizarreness or uniqueness. Even a patient with organic brain disease, as in senile degeneration or cerebral arteriosclerosis, is merely an individual who is attempting to meet the ordinary challenges of everyday life with fewer brain cells at his disposal.

Secondly, the one-genus postulate has important sociological connotations. It stresses that the differences between a Polynesian aborigine, a Central American sharecropper and a Chicago industrialist are insignificant in comparison with their basic similarities. The central problems of day-to-day existence which each of them faces are more alike than dissimilar. The one-genus postulate stretches beyond clinical mental health work; it is profoundly humanitarian.

Thirdly, the one-genus postulate has important bearings on therapy. It emphasizes that in therapy one person, designated the patient or client, works with another individual, termed the therapist, who has special training and knowledge in helping people with damaging past and current interpersonal and emotional experiences. There are no basic differences between these two persons; one is merely using his personality and particular training to aid the other. *They are both much more simply human than otherwise.*

SULLIVAN'S BOUNDARIES BETWEEN NORMALITY AND PSYCHIATRIC ILLNESS

Although this subject may at first glance seem hackneyed, Sullivan has some interesting things to say about it. His attention, of course, is always on what is occurring between the patient and the people around him. The boundaries are always *interpersonal,* and by their very nature define what a psychiatric illness is. We have delayed considering Sullivan's definition of psychiatric illness until after discussion of his concepts of the various clinical disorders. This gives his definition concrete meaning and avoids unsubstantiality and vagueness.

A psychiatric illness is a set of significant disruptions or distortions in the interpersonal fields between the patient and other people. It embraces the entire range of inappropriate or inadequate interpersonal relations. There are no rigid psychiatric disorders; they vary in nature and intensity in response to what is going on, and has gone on, in the patient's life. Healthy interpersonal relationships can improve the patient and unhealthy ones can worsen him. The scope of psychiatric dysfunctions extends from problems such as marital and child rearing difficulties to the extensive disruptions of interpersonal life we call psychoses.

A psychiatric disturbance is produced by the sick ways in which a person seeks to satisfy his interpersonal needs. It is molded by his past history and his ongoing interactions with people. The patient's *past* determines which particular interpersonal relationship or event precipitates his disorder, and his *future* expectations of relationships with people play a role in determining the kind of psychiatric difficulty he will have and how severe it will be. Events and relationships, therapeutically constructed or otherwise, which favorably alter his awareness of the *past* and *present,* and change his expectations of the *future,* facilitate movements toward health.

In some cases the patient senses that various interpersonal avenues are closed to him; he simply cannot make the adjustments necessary to enter them. The sick pattern into which he has drifted seems the only way to go on living, and he is more or less aware of this. In many instances, however, the emotionally upset person does not understand, or understands only in partial, warped ways the unsound features of his interpersonal patterns. He does not grasp the differences between his unhealthy behavior and the healthy behavior of those around him.

If the discussions of the various psychiatric disorders in the preceding chapters are reviewed, it will be seen how faithful Sullivan is *to this interpersonal concept of emotional illness*. Like all original thinkers, he strays from his principles at times, but he eventually checks himself and returns to his fundamental ways of looking at things.

Until he was middle-aged, Sullivan lamented at times that from one period to another he sometimes changed his ideas about personality development and the various forms of psychiatric illness. Eventually, however, he saw that this flexibility prevented him from getting stuck in rigid viewpoints which were limited or false. This flexibilty allowed him to evolve his ideas as he accumulated more clinical experience throughout his life. Failure to realize that Sullivan's concepts must be looked at in an evolutionary light has caused, in our opinion, grave errors in the ways in which his works have been posthumously edited and published, and this has much retarded the comprehension of what he did and the spread of his viewpoints.

Sullivan was one of the first persons to stress the now commonplace point that since a psychiatric disorder is defined as consisting of inadequate or inappropriate interpersonal relationships, consideration must at times be given to the cultural settings in which such relationships are inappropriate or inadequate. In setting the boundaries where normality ends and psychiatric difficulties begin it frequently is not enough merely to evaluate the patient; it is necessary to appraise his cultural setting. If a rural, orthodox Moslem woman shouts at her husband she may be in the early stages of schizophrenia; if a San Diego woman does not shout at her husband she may have a passive personality disorder.

Sullivan also emphasizes another factor to which only cursory lip service frequently is given. In order to evaluate a patient the participant-observing professional person must set up a relationship with him, and the nature of that relationship may influence the patient's responses to such an extent that it affects his diagnosis, or the lack of it. How the professional person behaves affects the kinds of data he gets from the patient and this plays a role in his psychiatric diagnosis. *The observer is inescapably involved in the diagnosis, and the act of getting data always modifies those data to some extent.* In a very simple example, an alert, refreshed interviewer who evaluates a patient at 9 o'clock in the morning may get quite different data than if he, tired and anxious to go home, interviews him at 6 o'clock in the afternoon. The ways in which the collection of data molds its nature is one more factor in what actually happens in setting the boundaries between normality and sickness.

This principle is quite similar to that of the 1932 Nobel laureate in physics, Werner Heisenberg. Heisenberg pointed out that because of the limitations of human beings as observers, and their necessary involvement in the processes they are observing, there are inevitable boundaries in their capacities to understand diverse physical phenomena. Heisenberg's principle is more complex than this, but these are its basic points. Sullivan feels the same is true in psychiatry. Neat distinctions between normality and abnormality are blurred to some extent by this factor, no matter what kinds of tools and situations are utilized. Diagnosis is always an interpersonal process.

How then does Sullivan briefly define a normal person?

Like most psychiatrists and other mental health professional workers, he quibbles over the use of the word normal. He dislikes employing it since everyone has at least minor emotional discomforts and interpersonal maladjustments from time to time. However, putting these objections aside, he lays down four criteria: 1) a well adjusted person has sound self-esteem. He feels he has value as a person; 2) he has a good level of emotional and interpersonal security. He has relatively little anxiety, and effective ways of coping with it when his interpersonal relationships are under strain; 3) he has broad capacities for forming good interpersonal relationships in a wide variety of settings; 4) as discussed in Chapter 7, he has a large spectrum of awareness of the nature and significance of his emotional and interpersonal functioning. A person has emotional health to the extent that he is aware of his interpersonal relationships. Sullivan's use of the word *awareness* must be understood in this connection; it is not cold knowledge, but a deeply imbued assimilation of feelings, ideas and attitudes, and a person's ability to bring these things into his focus of attention when his health demands it.

SOME COMMENTS ON VARIOUS KINDS
OF PERSONALITY MALFORMATIONS

Sullivan at no point in his lectures gives a systematic survey of those conditions which in the decades since his death have become labeled *personality disorders*. He taught and wrote extensively about only a few of these conditions, and he calls them *personality warps* or *personality malformations*.

In this section we shall gather together some material from Sullivan's teachings which are related to three aspects of personality disorders: 1) the interpersonal nature of a personality disorder, or malformation; 2) sociopathic, or asocial, personality malformations; 3) the interpersonal approach to persons who have homosexual adjustments. In no way do any of the following discussions constitute a systematic coverage of the subject, but Sullivan has valuable things to say on each of them. A few pearls may be of value even when there are not enough to make a necklace.

The Interpersonal Nature of a Personality Disorder, or Malformation. Sullivan feels that a personality disorder, or malformation, is a *persistent distortion* in the way a person deals with others. In contrast, neuroses and psychoses fluctuate much in intensity from one period to another, often last for only a specific period of time and then no longer influence the individual's functioning, and have features (such as an obsessive thought or a hysterical pain) that are not persistently interpersonal *in their direct clinical manifestations*. A personality malformation operates almost continually in the ways in which a person relates to the people around him. A person with an obsessive personality disorder, for example, is somewhat cold and mechanical in *all* his relationships at *all* times.

A personality malformation is composed of 1) unhealthy security operations (causing, in their totality, a defective self-system), 2) warped concepts of other people and oneself owing to unfavorable balances in the emotionally comfortable (good) me, the anxiety-ridden (bad) me, the emotionally comfortable (good) mother and father, and all the other forces outlined in our discussion of infancy, 3) impaired consensual validation, 4) parataxic distortions, 5) unhealthy dynamisms and 6) malfunctioning in all the other basic personality processes discussed at many places in this book. Some of these processes are much more prominent than others in a particular personality disorder, but they are all to some extent involved. The term personality disorder, or malformation, is therefore a *global term;* it describes a diffuse maldevelopment of the ways in which a person interacts with others.

The investigation of how all these forces operate to produce the various kinds of personality disorders offers a field of research for psychiatrists and other mental health professionals; it has to a large degree been neglected. We hope that the increase of interest in Sullivan's viewpoints in the 1970s and 1980s will lead to this work. Its implications for treatment will be extensive.

Sociopathic, or Asocial, Personality Malformations. Various nomenclatures employ diverse names for this group of personality disorders and divide it in special ways; the term antisocial personality disorder is commonly used for these persons, or a particular subgroup of them. The terminology utilized here is that of the American Psychiatric Association's Third Edition of its Diagnostic and Statistical Manual (DSM III), so that the nature of the patients being discussed will be clear. Our emphasis, of course, will be on the causes and nature of these difficulties as *interpersonal* processes.

The person with a sociopathic personality disorder never had, during his infancy, childhood, juvenile period and early adolescence, an interpersonal relationship in which he experienced tender acceptance, value as a person and meaningful intimacy. In many cases he was subjected to much hostility, depreciation and rejection. He emerges from these traumas without the capacity to establish healthy emotional commitments in others. Such commitments threaten him; he expects in them repetition of the innumerable incidents in which he was rejected and devalued.

As a result he does not make effective contacts with people. The events in which he is involved do not carry the impacts of meaningful experience; as far as his psychological development is concerned, it is as if the events did not occur, and hence, he learns nothing from them, Repeated interpersonal failures, or even calamities, do not cause him in adolescence and adulthood to modify his ways of living, since he has no emotional commitment in the people with whom he interacts. For him people are objects to be juggled, avoided or exploited as the circumstances of the moment dictate.

Some sociopathic persons become skillful in camouflaging their non-involvement behind façades of charm or garrulous camaraderie as means of achieving their ends as effortlessly as possible. This type of sociopathic person often causes much suffering and perplexity to his marital partner, work associates and others, and his effects on his developing children may be very damaging.

Other individuals with sociopathic personality malformations manifest, as a result of their traumatic formative years, open hostility and refusals to conform to the standards of the society in which they were reared. Chronic familial, vocational and social conflicts serve various interpersonal purposes for them. These conflicts prevent any true investments in other people, and thus allow them to avoid the emotional commitments which threaten them. Open conflicts also permit them to maintain some kind of vibrant interpersonal life, sick as it is, and this is more tolerable than isolation from people. Constant brawls, arguments and tricky maneuvers, self-defeating as they are, provide them with a means of avoiding the dreadful vacuum of interpersonal solitude. Moreover, these persons get an increase in self-esteem by the turmoil they cause; quarreling with others, and being entangled with them in deceit and fraud, imply that they are of sufficient value to be worth so much turbulence and trouble. However, since the added self-esteem has a hollow, transitory quality, they are constantly driven on to more antisocial behavior.

The Interpersonal Approach to Persons Who Have Homosexual Adjustments. Sullivan views homosexuality as an incomplete development; a homosexual person does not reach the full extent of his emotional and interpersonal capacities. Thus, to a certain extent, Sullivan sidesteps the issue of whether homosexuality is a pathological condition or an alternative form of sexual living. In this, as in many things,

Sullivan was considering in the 1920s and 1930s an issue that has come to the center of psychiatric attention in the 1970s and 1980s. Nevertheless, he feels that the person who attains a comfortable heterosexual adjustment achieves a richer life than the person who does not.

He feels that in many cases homosexuality is caused by a "misfortune in models." A close, but somewhat anxiety-tinged, relationship with the parent of the opposite sex combines with a distant or abrasive relationship with the parent of the same sex to make the role of the parent of the opposite sex a more comfortable one for the developing child. In such a case, for example, a boy finds his mother's outlook and orientation more inviting than his father's, and he runs a risk of drifting into it when the period for choosing sexual partners arrives; he chooses sexual partners a woman would choose, who are members of his own sex.

Sullivan rejects the concept that a person becomes homosexual because of a block against heterosexuality. That is, he does not accept the idea that a homosexual is a person who is uncomfortable, or frankly panicky, about physical genital activity with a person of the opposite sex and, as a second best adjustment, expresses his sexual urges in genital activities with persons of his own sex.

In Sullivan's opinion, a homosexual does not grow beyond the juvenile period, when most interpersonal activities are with persons of his own sex, into the stage of genital interest in persons of the opposite sex that characterizes adolescence and adulthood. He does not make this growth step because of the misfortune in models outlined above. A child of 10 months fails to talk not because of a block against talking, but because he has not yet grown to the interpersonal level of a three-year-old child who talks. This crude illustration makes clear Sullivan's concept of a failure of growth, rather than a block to growth, as the cause of homosexuality.

A heterosexual adjustment is much more likely when the growing person has a sound relationship with the parent of the same sex. This is particularly so when the parent of the same sex approves and encourages those activities which are culturally associated with their common sex. A sound relationship with the parent of the same sex should, of course, dovetail with a healthy, affectionate relationship with the parent of the opposite sex. These are the *interpersonal* determinants of a firm heterosexual orientation. Sullivan in all ways rejects Freud's dictum, "Anatomy is destiny." For him, "Interpersonal relationships are destiny."

Sullivan feels, moreover, than when a person, because of traumas affecting his sexual models during his developing years, arrives at the end of his juvenile period with wavering, confused sexual models, his final mode of sexual adjustment may be influenced by the kinds of close relationships he has with nonfamily persons of his own general age bracket. For example, if a close friendship occurs between an actively sexual adolescent and a juvenile of the same sex a few years younger than him, it may be contaminated by much homosexual genital activity. This, Sullivan feels may be sufficient to cast the person with unsure, confused sexual models into a homosexual adjustment.

A PARADIGM: THE INTERPERSONAL APPROACH
TO MENTAL RETARDATION

We shall conclude our consideration of the interpersonal approach to psychiatric disorders by examining Sullivan's views on mental retardation, a condition which many mental health professionals would not consider mainly interpersonal in nature. Sullivan disagrees. He feels that mental retardation presents a special set of challenges in working out a comfortable way of life, *but the things which cause trouble in mentally retarded persons are mainly the untoward interpersonal relationships that the person's learning difficulties set up between him and other people.*

We shall discuss mental retardation in terms of Sullivan's views on 1) the underlying defect and 2) the ways in which interpersonal relationships are affected by the underlying defect and thus produce the major problems of the retarded individual.

The Underlying Defect. Sullivan defines intelligence as the ability 1) to see the relatedness of things and 2) to use the conventionally accepted symbols of the person's culture.

The retarded person has more trouble than others in distinguishing the ways in which various things are similar and dissimilar, and in seeing how they are related or unrelated to each other. He also has special difficulties in learning to employ the innumerable symbols about him; language, gestures, abstract concepts and many other kinds of symbols give him more trouble than they do to other people.

However, his incapacity to see the similarities of things and to employ symbols is relatively small in terms of the entire spectrum of similarities and symbols in his culture. More than 95 percent of retarded persons fall in the categories of mild or moderate retardation, and in time they learn to speak, to understand the basic prohibitions which society imposes on its members and to conduct themselves in ways that are acceptable to the culture they live in.

Their major problems of life adjustment lie in an entirely different field, that of their interpersonal dealings with the people around them.

Mental Retardation as an Interpersonal Problem. The main difficulties of mentally retarded individuals arise from the fact that the people around them treat them as if they were basically different from others. The vast majority of them are *not* basically different; they differ in relatively minor ways, when the total field of interpersonal adjustment is considered.

This is exemplified in a small but important aspect of their behavior. If one enters a classroom of mentally retarded children, especially in an institutional setting, one is quickly struck by the fact that these children smile much less than other groups of children. Their faces tend to have a set, expressionless aspect. *They smile less because throughout their developing years other people did not smile much at them.* Their faces lack the mobility of the faces of other children because during infancy and childhood the people caring for them did not talk in animated ways with them. The facial expressions of their parents, siblings and others were dampened by the fact that these persons *knew that the child was retarded.* Put in simple terms, the problem was in the heads of the people caring for the retarded child and not *inside* the child himself. *The problem was interpersonal.*

If mentally retarded children are closely observed, a subtle physical ineptness is seen in the movements of their hands, arms, legs and bodies. This too is interpersonal in origin. During their formative years their fathers did not toss baseballs back and forth with them, include them in the routine tasks of the home, such as painting garage doors and putting up storm windows or play with them in animated ways. Mothers did not include them in making cakes, cookies and table decorations for birthday parties. Siblings did not integrate them into their games both inside and outside the home. As a result, they are not adroit in their physical actions. They have these features because people considered them different and set up distorted interpersonal relationships with them.

The world moves a little too fast for mentally retarded children, and the people around them, *thinking them different from others, treat them differently and exclude them from a wide range of interpersonal experience.* For the vast majority of retarded children, the time differential is small, but it has a large effect on what happens to them because of the attitudes of the people about them. Whereas a playmate is willing to wait a bit longer for a child he thinks of normal intelligence to put on a baseball glove or get something out of a drawer, he shunts the retarded child aside. Whereas a parent or a neighbor is willing to wait some time for a normal child to get dressed to go the supermarket, he decides not to wait for a retarded child. The child is thus deprived of interpersonal experience.

Close observation reveals that most retarded children whistle less, sing less lustily than their peers, and often do not sing when alone. They do so because people are more subdued in their presence and do not do these things when with them. Some retarded children have a subtle melancholy and a cautiousness in trying to do new things, and they are less vivacious in the use of expressions such as "okay," "thank you" and others. Their voices do not ring with customary childish pitches because they have grown up among people whose alacrity was deadened by their constant awareness that the child was retarded.

All these things, and many similar ones, are well established by the time the child begins grade school, and often they are evident at three or before. Hence, when he goes out into the broader world of the neighborhood, the schoolroom and the playground *interpersonal forces have already made him a less attractive person.* As a result, children shy away from him and he is deprived from the alert give-and-take with other children which could help to repair the interpersonal damage already done. In school he is often secluded along with other children who have undergone the same process, or is treated with neglect or patronizing condescension. Interpersonal forces, not his underlying retardation, mold him and predispose him to whatever social problems he may have.

There are, in addition, the more devastating misadventures which his retardation may cause such as parental rejection, parental over-protectiveness, public ridicule, a tendency by the family to hide him from view under the guise of "protecting" him, sexual and vocational exploitation by unprincipled individuals and many other untoward experiences.

The adverse interpersonal consequences of this treatment may, in time, seem to make the attitudes of others justified. The child's sullenness, or fearful withdrawal, or rebelliousness, or timid inability to profit from experience are cited as justifications for past treatment, present mishandling and future pessimism. Sullivan's principles of reciprocal emotions, outlined in Chapter 7, applies in a special way to retarded children, adolescents and adults.

In brief, Sullivan feels that the dominant behavioral characteristics of the retarded person are usually the products of the *interpersonal processes which occur because other people consider him to be retarded; in the strict sense, these emotional and interpersonal characteristics have very little to do with the retardation itself.*

The implications of these views in terms of treatment, education of the public, and total life planning for each retarded person are vast.

This interpersonal examination of retardation provides us with a format for looking at a wide range of other conditions. However, in his psychiatric career, which lasted only a little more than a quarter of a century, Sullivan did no more than make random observations on some of these areas. In a book that aims to do no more than present the work he actually did, we shall go no further.

The possibilities for objective, scientific study of interpersonal processes are much greater today than in Sullivan's time owing to marked advances in technological equipment. The relatively crude recording devices of Sullivan's era have been replaced by much more sophisticated equipment. Marked advances have been made in tape recorders and in audiovisual instruments. Physiological responses to interpersonal events can be recorded by devices at some distance from the person and not physically connected to him. A panoply of tools for investigating what occurs between people has been evolved and is continually being expanded. The transistor and the electronic chip have revolutionized methods for observing human interactions, and the recording, storing and retrieving of data are being continually refined. It is quite possible that Sullivan, in time, will be viewed as a psychiatric pioneer whose viewpoints required several decades of technological advances before the truly scientific nature of his work could be firmly established.

Bibliography

Many psychiatrists and other mental health professionals find Sullivan's works difficult to read. This is to a large extent owing to the fact that the bulk of his material now in book form comes from transcribed lectures and seminars that were tape-recorded during the last several years of his life. Each book assumes that the reader is familiar with many terms and concepts that are defined elsewhere and not in the volume the person is reading.

In an attempt to prepare mental health professionals to read Sullivan's work with easy comprehensibility, we have in recent years published two other books on the subject. They are, in order of publication, *Harry Stack Sullivan: His Life and His Work,* and *The Treatment Techniques of Harry Stack Sullivan.*

The first of these books contains in its first chapter a detailed biographical sketch of Sullivan. It pays special attention to the features of Sullivan's education and clinical experience which influenced his literary style in ways that often cause difficulties to readers; a similar chapter, with particular attention to material on Sullivan's teaching methods, forms the last chapter of the second book. The rest of the first book offers a bird's eye view of all aspects of Sullivan's work. The second book of this series focuses on Sullivan's therapeutic techniques.

These two volumes end with book-by-book annotated bibliographies of the eight volumes in which Sullivan's published material is available; the valuable sections and the weak parts of each book are noted in detail. Six of these books by Sullivan are out in paperback form.

For persons with a special interest in Sullivan, two further points are worth noting.

The William Alanson White Foundation of Washington, D.C. drew up, in 1974, a definitive, 14-page bibliography of everything Sullivan published. It includes even such minor items as book reviews he wrote and discussions he gave on papers delivered by other persons at psychiatric meetings. This

191

bibliography can be obtained from the William Alanson White Psychiatric Foundation, Inc., 1610 New Hampshire Avenue, N.W., Washington, D. C. 20009.

Mental health professionals sometimes place in their offices and studies photographs of distinguished psychiatrists and other mental health pioneers whose work they value. So far as is known, Sullivan only once in his life sat for a series of portrait style photographs. These were made by the well known photographer Margaret Bourke-White, a former patient of his. At present there is only one source for one of these fine photographs. For a modest fee it can be ordered from the New York Academy of Medicine, 2 East 103rd Street, New York, N. Y. 10029.

BLITSTEN, D. R. (Ed.). *The Social Theories of Harry Stack Sullivan*. New York: The William Frederick Press, 1953.

BRUCH, H. Interpersonal theory: Harry Stack Sullivan. In: Burton, A. (Ed.), *Operational Theories of Personality*. New York: Brunner/ Mazel, 1974.

CHAPMAN, A. H. *Harry Stack Sullivan: His Life and His Work*. New York: G. P. Putnam's Sons, 1976.

CHAPMAN, A. H. *The Treatment Techniques of Harry Stack Sullivan*. New York: Brunner/Mazel, 1978.

CHAPMAN, A. H., DAVIS, J. M., and ALMEIDA, E. M. *Textbook of Clinical Psychiatry. An Interpersonal Approach*. Second Edition. Philadelphia: J. B. Lippincott, 1976.

CHRZANOWSKI, G. *Interpersonal Approach to Psychoanalysis. Contemporary View of Harry Stack Sullivan*. New York: Halsted Press, 1977.

HAVENS, L. L. *Approaches to the Mind*. Boston: Little, Brown, 1973. Chapters 5 and 10.

KVARNES, R. G. and PARLOFF, G. H. (Eds.). *A Harry Stack Sullivan Case Seminar*. New York: W. W. Norton, 1976.

MULLAHY, P. (Ed.). *A Study of Interpersonal Relations*. New York: Hermitage House, 1967.

MULLAHY, P. (Ed.). *The Contributions of Harry Stack Sullivan*. New York: Hermitage Press, 1952.

MULLAHY, P. *Psychoanalysis and Interpersonal Psychiatry*. New York: Science House, 1970.

NOBLE, D. and BURNHAM, D. L. *A History of the Washington Psycho-*

analytic Society. Washington, D.C.: The Washington Psychoanalytic Society, 1969.

SULLIVAN, H. S. *Conceptions of Modern Psychiatry.* New York: W. W. Norton, 1953.

SULLIVAN, H. S. *The Interpersonal Theory of Psychiatry.* New York: W. W. Norton, 1953.

SULLIVAN, H. S. *The Psychiatric Interview.* New York: W. W. Norton, 1954.

SULLIVAN, H. S. *Clinical Studies in Psychiatry.* New York: W. W. Norton, 1956.

SULLIVAN, H. S. *Schizophrenia as a Human Process.* New York: W. W. Norton, 1962.

SULLIVAN, H. S. *The Fusion of Psychiatry and Social Science.* New York: W. W. Norton, 1964.

SULLIVAN, H. S. *Personal Psychopathology.* New York: W. W. Norton, 1972.

WITENBERG, E. G. (Ed.). *Interpersonal Explorations in Psychoanalysis.* New York: Basic Books, 1973, Introduction, Chapter 7 and Chapter 13.

Index

Adolescence. *See also* Preadolescence
  and adequate adulthood, 88-89
  duration of, 2
  dynamisms in, 81-86, 93-97
    characteristic, 84
  early/late, 74, 78
  intimacy in, 76-79
  obsessive-compulsion in, 127
  personality growth in, 74-76
  personality problems in, 58, 86-88
  psychotherapy in, 90-93, 97-99
  and security operations, 84
  sexuality, lust, intimacy in, 3, 76-79
Alcoholism, 110
All-Giving Mother, 7. *See also* Mother
American Psychiatric Association, 182
Anesthesia, 144
Antipsychotic medications, 113, 146, 161
Antisocial personality, 49
Anxiety states, viii, 30-31, 99, 101, 103-
    11, 132
  and adulthood, 89
  causes of, interpersonal, 76, 104-107
  in childhood, 51-53
  consequences of, interpersonal, 107-109
  defined, 11
  and disjunctive force, 107
  diverse outgrowths of, 110-11
  gradient of, 22-23
  and group association, 60
  and hostility, 109
  in infancy, 20-23, 104
  and interpersonal event, 21-22
  management of, 51-52
  and needs, 24
  and parents, 16
  and psychic accessibility, 65
  and psychosis, 146-47

  and security operations, 22, 57
  and self, 18, 37, 92
  sexual, 84, 86
  and therapy, 5, 93, 98
Aphonia, 144
Archetypes, Jungian, 7, 14, 33
Arteriosclerosis, cerebral, 177
Authority figures, 41
Autism in infancy, 27-29
Awareness/unawareness:
  and anxiety, 63, 107-108
  juvenile period, 63-65
  and therapy, 91

Bacon, Francis, 14
Blocking, schizophrenic, 156

Catatonic schizophrenia, 153-54. *See also*
    Schizophrenia
Cathexes, 84
Chapman, A. H., vii-ix
Chapman, Miriam C. M. S., ix
Character disorders, 101
Childhood, 30-45
  anxiety in, 51-53
  consensual validation in, 41-45
  duration of, 3
  interpersonal relationships in, 30-32
  parataxic experience in, 39-41, 49-50
  personality evolution in, 32-33
  personality integration in, 80
  psychotherapy in, 46-49
  and relative attention, 83
  and schizophrenia, 146-48
  security operations development in, 33-
    36
  self-system origins in, 36-39

195